THE FALSE DIALECTIC
BETWEEN
CHRISTIANS AND ATHEISTS

THE FALSE DIALECTIC BETWEEN CHRISTIANS AND ATHEISTS

TOM DONOVAN

Algora Publishing
New York

Library of Congress Cataloging-in-Publication Data —

Donovan, Tom, 1967–
Title: The false dialectic between Christians and atheists / Tom
    Donovan.
Description: New York : Algora Publishing, 2016. | Includes bibliographical
    references and index.
Identifiers: LCCN 2016030985 (print) | LCCN 2016031121 (ebook) | ISBN
    9781628942101 (soft cover : alk. paper) | ISBN 9781628942118 (hard cover :
    alk. paper) | ISBN 9781628942125 (pdf)
Subjects: LCSH: Philosophy and religion. | Religion—Philosophy. |
    Religion—Controversial literature. | Socrates. | Descartes, Rene,
    1596–1650. | Marx, Karl, 1818-1883. | Sartre, Jean-Paul, 1905–1980.
Classification: LCC BL51 .D564 2016 (print) | LCC BL51 (ebook) | DDC 210—dc23 LC
record available at https://lccn.loc.gov/2016030985

Cover illustration by Wendy Walczak.

Printed in the United States

For Christine and Thomas

Four philosophers walk into heaven (don't ask where they are walking from). Right away Socrates starts asking questions. He asks those at the gates if they know what the Form of Heaven is, the Form through which this particular heaven is participating. Descartes crosses himself and thanks God for finally disposing of his crummy body. It's no fun being sick all the time and without a body Descartes feels light. But he can't figure out why he still has a cough. Marx looks around and is appalled at the class structure of this place. Hierarchies everywhere! He notices that angels are divided into those who have wings and those who do not, with only about 1% having wings. He's ready to write a new manifesto but wonders if critiquing heaven is an ideological mistake. Isn't heaven merely part of the superstructure? Sartre stands tall, but is still short. He claims not to be afraid and he says God has some explaining to do. "I'm still a man, damn it!" he yells, while at the same time glancing around nervously, hoping he doesn't run into any of those many women he lied to.

Table of Contents

Chapter 1. I'm Nothing

1

Why do even stupid jokes about heaven or hell still make us smile, or frighten us, offend us, provoke arguments amongst us, and make us dream, debate, and denounce? Will we ever shake our Judeo-Christian origins? Why hasn't philosophy replaced religion, and why hasn't philosophy grown beyond a reactionary atheism? Despite its failure, could it be that philosophy is a cure for religion and even for atheism? The true philosophical urge is an anti-metaphysical urge. Philosophy is against theism and atheism. And it's definitely against agnosticism. These claims may seem counterintuitive as philosophy is generally considered, in large part, to be a search for metaphysical truth. It's considered a discipline rooted in the search for eternal truths, and when the truth is unclear, philosophy is expected to embrace modesty and have a willingness to say "I don't know."

Philosophy began against religion and against atheism. It began against religion as it tried to understand the world without appealing to gods. Thales is the model here: "The earth rests on water."[1] It began against atheism because it tried to understand the world without rejecting the gods, without rejecting the transcendent. Again, Thales is the model: "All things are full of gods."[2] The gods were considered to be around, or perhaps everywhere, so to speak, but for philosophy types they were mainly seen as an epiphenomenon when it came to human things. But, of course, it's more complicated than that. For the Ancient

---

1 Aristotle, *The Basic Works of Aristotle* (*Metaphysics* 983b18).
2 Ibid. (*De Anima* 411a7).

Greeks sometimes the supernatural was brought in to explain origins (think of Anaximander's The Boundless), to unify or ground like skyhooks, or was used as metaphor for nature and causality. Sometimes the gods were flat-out rejected or ignored. Sometimes the gods were central. It was occasionally more than hinted at that they were merely fictions; sometimes it was asserted that they were unnecessary or unknowable, and on occasion it was thought that they were quite bad or indifferent.

But the point is, for Ancient Greek philosophy, the truth about the gods was not directly of concern, and it was rarely an indirect concern. Philosophy cared about and aimed for human things, such as the pleasure of understanding, happiness, excellence, virtue, and success. It was not about abstract beliefs; it was much more focused on concrete actions. Belief in God and its foil atheism, though, are centrally about belief. Both then are against philosophy even as they walk along beside it; sometimes we embrace and stand near that which we are against. Agnosticism is even more against philosophy since it hasn't even gotten to the level of belief yet.

But really why is it so hard to cast off religion and/or transcend atheism? Why are we still talking about metaphysics? Some people argue that the fact that religion has been around for so long, and has not gone away, means that it must be true. Well, atheism has been around for thousands of years too. But lasting a long time is not a sign of truth. It's a sign of endurance. And really, what has gone away? Not war, sexism, racism, torture, or greed. Perhaps the longevity of religion and atheism should count against both. Perhaps both are forms of avoidance behavior. It's easier to focus on belief than it is to take up a new practice of living. Fixation concerning belief in God — a focus on metaphysics — serves the ruling class interests and feeds society's mode of production. Nonetheless, shouldn't we be past this tired dualism?

2

Perhaps not. Metaphysical questions still haunt us. The latest Woody Allen movie, *Irrational Man*, begins with the line: "Kant said human reason is troubled by questions that it cannot dismiss but also cannot answer." Questions about the ultimate meaning and nature of the universe abound within us still. But similar to Allen's not so great movie, the questions and answers have lost their charm. There is something really pathetic about being religious today, as there is something uninspiring about being an atheist. If we cannot move on, then perhaps we too are losing our charm. If Kant is correct that the metaphysical urge, the urge to understand the nature of the universe and our place in it, is a desire we necessarily feel and unfortunately cannot answer or satisfy, then the charm of being human may be coming to an end. If we remain stuck asking the same questions, or lose interest without finding deeper questions, we will cease to be; we will no longer exist in any meaningful sense. People who never grow up eventually are not taken seriously anymore. At some point, if we keep repeating ourselves, not necessarily just the second time, history, our history, will become farce. Fortunately, at some level, each of us must reproduce for ourselves what it means to be human. We need not stay stuck with the same beliefs or in the same situations and choices forever. Our identities need not conform to or be limited by reified beliefs. We have the potential to transcend false beliefs and in doing so create deeper and more meaningful lives. Even the metaphysical urge is not a timeless universal urge; as the self is not a timeless universal entity. Rather, at this moment of history, we are *unformed*, for we live in a free society and our choices are many. In this book we will take a journey, with dialectical philosophy as our guide, in the hope that we can form ourselves, with will and consciousness, into something greater, into something better. We can form ourselves, and make ourselves and the people who matter proud. The urge to make ourselves and the people who matter proud is a more profound urge than the abstract urge to affirm or deny God. It's a more mature urge whose day has come. It's time to move into the post-Woody Allen phase of our humanity.

3

But what does it mean to be post-metaphysical? It clearly has something to do with abandoning religion, but it is more than that. In even the Western mind there are various, seemingly endless, versions of being religious. But at the base what does it mean to have a religious way of looking at the world? There is no one answer. Perhaps, for the Western mind, this way predominantly encourages us to try to connect with a supernatural being. Meaning and value are thought to come from supernatural creatures, or one supernatural being. The goal is to connect to something outside us and higher than us. If we extend things eastward, we can say that even Buddhism, although godless, attempts to connect the human with an essentially greater or truer world. It tries to show us that all suffering is rooted in desire, and that desire is linked to attachment. In reaction to this metaphysical assumption, the Buddhist way is to give up attachment and with it desire. This way one will come to see that the notion of an individual self is a fiction, and that ultimately one should seek to destroy the untrue self for the truth of Nirvana.

A secular version of the metaphysical urge is to believe that meaning and value don't come from God but come from Truth. This is the way of traditional philosophy. Socrates was the first important mind to articulate this. Some truth seekers are atheists, and some try to link truth with God, God as Truth. All these paths are filled with tricky puzzles, contradictions, intriguing answers, hopes, dreams, consistencies and inconsistencies. But the point is they all share a desire, a wish, or perhaps a need, to transcend the buzzing, blooming, contingent human realm for something outside or above us. They all seek to find an absolute truth and an objective reality to conform to. If this is the point, then even atheism shares in this metaphysical urge, with its need to assert that God does not exist.

4

Atheists who desire to discover absolute truth and objective reality without God reveal their affinity to theists. The affinity is more than an agreement on the nature of the metaphysical quest — God either exists or does not exist. It is also an existential covenant concerning meaning and value. Theists find meaning and value in God; atheists find meaning and value in the world, or they concede that meaning and values don't exist since there is no God. In this way both theists and atheists gain salvation and consolation, even if only negatively, from belief in a truth supposedly out there. Saying that God does not exist, and therefore concluding that no one — or no thing — can save us, is itself a type of liberation and existential salvation. In all these cases the existential riddle involves metaphysical transcendence; the answer to the human condition is something outside us that nonetheless determines us. This type of thinking is dualistic, but not symmetrical, in two senses. First the dualism between what's "out there" and us assumes priority to what's supposedly outside us. Second, the dualism between believers and non-believers tilts toward the believers. In the first case what's really out there holds all the cards, and we have to accept its hand and try to conform to it or reject it at our own peril; and in the second, theists hold all the cards, and atheists have to either accept or reject the theists' hand. In this way the game is rigged twice. First, by the way the world supposedly is, despite us, and second, by theists, since atheists are defined by a negative principle, by what atheists are not (atheists are not believers). The absence of God sets the conditions in which atheists live their lives, for who atheists think they are.

5

We should reject both these dualisms. We need not just assume there is a world out there independent of us, for we are part of the world. And we need not accept the label of atheist, for we are not simply defined by our non-beliefs. We can begin to understand new possibilities when we look at the fact that some atheists, besides obviously rejecting God, also decenter the pursuit of a true world independent of us; in other words, they just give up on, move beyond, abstract metaphysical questions. Nietzsche's version of existentialism rejects God and the search for external truth in favor of the claim that meaning and value are something to be created rather than discovered. The idea here is that rather than spending one's life chasing God or Truth, or reacting against them, one should engage in thoughtful actions that make life meaningful and that give value to one's life. The goal is not to try to conform to the world nor make the whole world conform to one's beliefs; rather the goal is to create oneself into someone special, someone excellent, someone virtuous, someone successful, someone you and those who matter can be proud of. This attitude does not turn belief into a fetish. It does not turn truth into a fetish. It does not reduce individuals to what they happen to believe. It doesn't view true belief as a stagnant correspondence with external reality. Rather it understands that beliefs arise from concrete and creative actions, are intertwined with them, and change as human practices change. Further this view understands that a belief's justification comes through language and dialogue. And dialogue only happens within and between other people, so there is no attempt or need to transcend beyond us or escape to something outside us. When one makes this move the theoretical Kantian questions, and specifically the idea of either God or no-God, falls apart and becomes uninteresting. And at this point in history simply claiming to be religious or merely claiming to be an atheist is uninteresting.

6

Yet many who walk along Nietzsche's path of prioritizing action, creation, and interpretation somewhat still miss the point and cling to the idea of atheism, thinking it refutes God while it actually weds them to God. Clinging to atheism is a distraction and a misunderstanding, once we recognize that meaning and value only exist as creations by us. The implication is that it is a category mistake to continue to use a term that is predicated on meaning and value being out there to be discovered. There is nothing to be discovered. Those looking for the supernatural will never find it. Rejecting the label "atheist" signals recognition of the misguided quest for the supernatural. By rejecting the label, one rejects the metaphysics of discovery. This is a condition to turn one's attention to a better quest. The better quest is to focus on creating meaning and value. Nietzsche elegantly buried the idea of God, and if someone in the modern world is religious today, it is tempting to think it is out of willful ignorance.

No modern, sane person can seriously believe in monotheism. People today don't truly believe that God is constantly watching them, and everyone else, right now. If they did, they would also have to believe that God watches when an innocent child is tortured, raped, and murdered. And don't say that God doesn't like that that happens but that God has to respect free will. Look, almost all of us believe in free will, and yet if any of us see another torturing and raping a child, we are going to put a stop to it immediately. We are not going to wait until some future time to set the world right, and neither would a God. Clearly, we know the truth, but something else is going on that is preventing many from admitting it. Monotheism is akin to mononucleosis. The latter is spread through saliva, but it is more comforting to say through kissing; the former is spread by charlatans, but it's more comforting to think it's through grace.

7

A bit more should be said about Nietzsche at this point. It's well known that Nietzsche used the idea of the eternal recurrence, as well as the metaphor of the camel, lion, and child, to challenge a linear way of thinking about human life.[1] A traditional Western mind thinks of human life as having a beginning, middle, and end. Add a believer to this and a human life is justified, a life is meaningful, if and when the individual goes to heaven. The implication here is that none of us knows if our life has meaning until after we die. The meaning and the value of one's life is discovered after death. Nietzsche understood how absurd this belief is, and he offered the idea of the eternal recurrence to counter it. The idea of the eternal recurrence is to give weight to lived existence, to give the present moment adequate heaviness. Otherwise one suffers in the same way as Tereza and Tomas in Kundera's sublime novel *The Unbearable Lightness of Being*. If we can imagine that we must live our exact lives over and over again, then each moment carries heaviness within it, intrinsically. This perspective could prompt us to seize our lives in their concrete unfolding and avoid the tragedy of a wasted life. Rather than floating through existence, or waiting to die to know if your life meant anything, you could attempt to experience each moment of concrete life as deeply and as meaningfully as possible with the motivating principle that if you were to live again, the exact same life, it would be rich and meaningful each time.

But Nietzsche also realized that life goes in cycles and experiencing the weight of existence can become a burden. Living deeply, caring, and creating meaning carries the opposite problem of a life lived lightly. The problem of a non-serious life is that nothing matters, so nothing sticks to you. The problem of a serious life is that everything matters, so everything sticks to you. In this latter case, sometimes, no matter what you do, your life will feel like a burden, or at least aspects of your life will. When you are carrying the

1 See *Thus Spake Zarathustra.*

things, so to speak, that life has given you or that you care about, it can feel rewarding — or it can become a burden. In either case, though, if you are carrying it, you are the camel. A camel can carry a lot of weight and doesn't need much water to travel far. It can be good to be a camel. At some point though, the camel will give out. Carrying one's traditions, family duties, or nation's expectations, and so on, can be life affirming; and sometimes it can begin to destroy you. When it starts to destroy you, rather than giving in to lightness, Nietzsche says you must become the lion. The lion says no, the lion will not carry the load anymore, for it has become an unbearable burden. The lion roars and rebels. But one cannot live forever in opposition, either. At some point one will fall back into what one was trying to escape, unless one can move beyond a reactive stance. We see people try to get beyond religion and we see them fall back into it like a beaten dog with its tail between its legs. It's hard to give up religion if you have nothing positive to replace it with. Atheism, in our world, is the lion. It says no to God. This is good, but ultimately one must become the child, or one will fall back into carrying the burden one had earlier tried to escape. Unlike the lion that wants to lash out and bite, the child forgets the burden. The child cannot take the burden seriously because the child has moved on to something better. The child says "yes" to life, to concrete life. The child only looks light from the outside, but the child lives in the present, takes in the present with all the seriousness of a good old playground kickball game, and exhausts the moment in its realness. It's recess and nothing else matters but the game; the game is reality. It's the youngster's job, at that moment, to exercise, socialize, and compete. In fifteen minutes everyone will be back in the classroom, so the moment must be seized. The child's beliefs may seem light, since it's only a game, but nonetheless, the child's actions and focus are dead serious. Unconcerned with detached and abstract beliefs, a child cannot take the religion of the adults seriously and is too interested in living life to even say "no" to what is silly and unimportant, for it means nothing, it is nothing, and the child is indifferent to it.

8

Those who know how silly the idea of God is need not bother with religion anymore. Granting the belief and the words of the believer any space in your consciousness will just make you worse off, as when playing basketball with players who are really bad at basketball. Being on the court with them just makes your game bad. The wise thing is to not play with them at all. Get off the court entirely — abandon the word "atheist." An Atheist (A/theist) needs a God to be against, and religion needs non-believers or at least the idea of a non-believer; it needs the contrast of the chosen and the unchosen.

Philosophy, though, needs neither. Philosophy is not first and foremost about belief (beliefs are ideological), so any theory that makes belief (either pro or con) foundational is not good philosophy. Philosophy is a thoughtful action that, when played correctly, dissolves God and atheism by dropping them in Thales-like water: water that dissolves reified notions and exposes their contingent, human history. Yet philosophy has been living in the desert for a very long time; the only way to get to the water is by taking a genealogical journey through our philosophical practices to purge ourselves of mystified notions. The journey is long, but at least the path is strewn with the charm of Socrates, Descartes, Marx, and Sartre.

9

Words are important, language is a power, and we will see that clinging to terms such as "atheism" encourages clinging to a misguided view of philosophy and a misguided understanding of what it means to be human today. The language of atheism is problematic. Rather than walking the path of atheism or the path of God, we need to find a new path; we need to create many new paths. Still, to reject both atheism and God is not something that should be taken lightly. Although God does not show up in any sense in which we are used to agents showing up and communicating, many still find comfort in believing God is watching them or communicating with them. But since beliefs are ideological, we need to test them against reality, against actions. The problem is that God does not speak nor visit us in any meaningful sense in which we normally think of speaking and visiting. Your kids either speak to you or visit you, or they do not. You might believe, well, they are thinking of me and visiting me in their thoughts; but in reality we all know that this is vastly different than actually talking to you and seeing you. In the real sense, then, God does not speak or visit. To be blunt: God will not speak to you. God will speak to no one. Therefore, we know we have no relationship with God, if having a relationship means there is dialogue. Dialogue requires mutual speaking and listening. You might pretend that you know Olivia Pope because you watch her on television, but you don't have a relationship with her. You might talk and listen to her through the television but she does not listen to you nor talk to you — she doesn't exist. And until God shows up to the conversation, we know that there is no relationship with God. As long as you are of sound mind, you know that you have no relationship with God any more than you do with Olivia Pope, or any one you can't talk to or visit with. In this sense we can say that rationally we know supernatural beings don't exist in relationships with us, in the manner that we define a relationship between supposedly communicative beings. God is not communicative. God has no language. God has never bothered to learn our language. As Jhumpa Lahiri says in *In Other Words*, "Because in the end to learn a language, to feel connected to it, you have to have a dialogue, however childlike, however imperfect."[1]

If you want to define having a relationship with God differently, for example you read signs in the world to be signs from God, or you believe God is talking to you in your mind, that's fine. But keep in mind this is not an appropriate use of the word "relationship" in the way that you really want a relationship with God or anyone else. People don't want to be in a relationship with someone who does not engage them in dialogue nor even speak to them, or visit them, or interact with them. The onus is on believers to defend or explain their relationship with God, to explain how the lack of communication, absence of dialogue, leads to any understanding. God has not spoken, written, texted, tweeted, or even gestured. In any other context, to claim to understand an agent (in this case a supernatural agent) without any communication from this supposed agent is just immaturity.

10

Still, to say that God does not exist is not to say that God can be easily done away with. God, whether God actually exists or not, has staying power. God, you have to respect. To get beyond God, we need to analyze and understand what God really means to us and for us. The concept "God" and the practice of religion carry valuable human importance. Historically, they are an important part of us and our ability to give our lives meaning and value. They are not to be thoughtlessly or immaturely discarded.

God, gods, religion, and the supernatural have an important history that we don't want to simply throw away. Human understanding is rooted in history, and much of the beauty and truth of life is embedded even in discredited ideologies. Max Horkheimer, in *Eclipse of Reason*, emphasizes that modern society underestimates how older forms of life hold many current things up, how our ideological history is responsible for the intrinsic enjoyment of many things. "The pleasure of keeping a garden goes back to ancient times when gardens belonged to the gods and were cultivated from them. The sense of beauty in both nature and art is connected, by a thousand delicate threads, to these old superstitions. If, by either flouting or flaunting the threads, modern man cuts them, the pleasure may continue for a while but its inner life is extinguished."[2] He continues: "We cannot credit our enjoyment of a flower or of the atmosphere of a room to an autonomous

---

1 Jhumpa Lahiri, *In Other Words*, Ann Goldstein, tr. (Alfred A. Knopf, New York 2015) 25.
2 All of my quotations in this section from Horkheimer are from his *Eclipse of Reason* 24–5.

esthetic instinct." In other words, our sense of beauty, goodness, and truth is intimately connected to a prehistory of reverence. Some sense of sacredness or inherent goodness in the things we love precedes the enjoyment of the beauty we find in them. This even applies to concepts such as freedom, justice, and equality. "Such ideas must preserve the negative element, as the negation of the ancient stage of injustice or inequality, and at the same time conserve the original absolute significance rooted in their dreadful origins. Otherwise they become not only indifferent but untrue."

If we give up God, gods, religion, and the supernatural without reflection, without dialectically transcending them, we will lose more than we gain. Even consciously giving up something we know we should give up can cause suffering. Baudelaire called it "spleen." We might call it the feeling of melancholy when we still have love of something despite it losing its significance in the world. Some things still hold intrinsic worth for us and we will continue to care for them, but it hurts, we feel the spleen, because it no longer makes practical or rational sense for us to hold on to these things. These things no longer hold their prior worth in the world. We experience spleen knowing that what we love is untrue or lost forever. Yet we still hold and cherish them along with the melancholy, even if and perhaps partly because we know they are untrue. We feel this deeply when a relationship or tradition dies. Many people continue to experience spleen intensely today, especially during the holidays. Our traditions have lost their simple truths, yet admitting they are false is often too much. The alternative seems worse. To lose the deep joy and meaning from the activities, events, and moments connected to one's spiritual beliefs seems too high a price to pay, regardless of their truth value. Giving up all the beauty, community, and meaning, only to replace all that with ordinary hobbies, sports, shopping, television, and such, is a bad deal. It's an affront to one's identity and forces one to rethink certain practices. The unhappy consequence of giving up religion is real, and something that must be taken seriously, and dealt with practically. There is something noble about those who have refused to completely give up their religion out of spleen. Nobler still are those who have redefined their traditions to hold on to what they can without becoming willfully stupid. It's a difficult balance but it is admirable, more so than refusing to face the truth of the past, and discarding the past thoughtlessly. History's dialectic, though, will even outwit those who think they can cast off the past without consequence. Even those who think they have given it up without hurt betray themselves when we look closely at their faces. Those who become completely cynical end up in a Madame Bovary-like state of ennui.

Conscious of it or not, the truth of our rootedness in history is embedded in our bodies. Many people, rather than allowing themselves to feel the spleen, have given in to distraction, hobbies, good times, and fun with no regret over the loss of historical meaning. It seems that, for a lot of Americans, drinking wine and beer is today's way of sublimating, for dealing with all that is lost but which cannot be acknowledged. Horkheimer points out that in the Ancient world "good humor" was related to divinity. It carries into today as we try to project a healthy outlook even when we are feeling sick, broken, and lost. The recollection inside our bones outs the mask on our face; it shows on us as we try to put on a good face — pronounce that we "feel great!" — repeat PMA (positive mental attitude) — blurt out "I'm blessed" — sing "I will be happy today even if skies are grey" — until the desperation seeps out through the voice and the pinched facial muscles explode off the face. It's especially tough in the States, for this country demands a positive attitude, whether it's merited or not: no one should show weakness, no one is allowed to be down. And yet we see the downside too often when we look around and everywhere witness the forced smiles of people hiding their existential fears and lack of "good humor." The mantras "keep smiling" and "fake it till you make it" capture the deep feeling of spleen festering within those in line at the grocery store, in school, at church, walking through the mall, driving on the highway, at work, at the reunion, during the holiday, and at the game. We even see the consequences of this within modern religions today. One of the losses in the move from Catholicism to Protestantism was a loss of continuity in the Christian tradition. Some versions of Protestantism have tried to compensate for this loss by turning faith into a fetish. It creates a type of dogmatism evident in the frenzied approach of many Protestants when juxtaposed to the nonchalance emanating from Catholics grounded in over a thousand years of history and tradition of spirituality. The unconscious doubt, sadness, and despair, subtly yet clearly exposed through the forced smile and slightly off-pitch voice, are a sight and sound no one enjoys.

11

It's tough then, because one pays an existential price even if one abandons an untrue past. Untrue or not, it gave meaning and significance that cannot easily be washed off. But beyond the existential price, does it make sense logically both to say there is no such thing as God, and that atheism is irrational and false? Existential angst aside, doesn't it have to be one or the other? Either there are supernatural beings or there are not. It doesn't seem that complicated. Really, what could be beyond God or atheism? Nothing. In the United States you often hear the question — Are you a Christian or an atheist? — Neither, I'm nothing.[1] I'm neither a sinner nor a saint. I'm not passively natural or blessedly supernatural. I'm not otherworldly idealist or

---

1 I owe Wendy Walczak for this articulation.

mechanistic materialist. I'm neither chaste nor a fornicator. I'm not for you or against you, not witch or warlock, not black or white, not holy or unholy, not Kobe or Shaq, not sacred or profane, not vampire or werewolf, not theist or atheist.

Accepting the term "atheist" is like accepting the term "fornication." If you go out this weekend and, as the kids say, "hook up" or "get lucky," you need not accept the label of fornicator. It doesn't make you that just because someone calls you that. You are nothing; you just had a good weekend. If someone were to accuse you of being a fornicator, you would just look at that person as if that person were an idiot. That person would be an idiot. In the same way, if you do not worship supernatural beings, there really shouldn't be a word for it. There's only a word for it because the kooks have been controlling the discourse for a really long time. If you don't believe in God, then you are just normal, sane, and correct. You are nothing. The believer's fiction doesn't mean anything to you; you are, perhaps, just amused.

Rejecting a negative label, an anti-label, can create new possibilities. For example, someone might label you "anti-social" or "rude" because you don't like parties and loud events and activities. But you are not anti-social; you are not rude. You are an introvert. When we let extroverts control the discourse, we miss the deeper beauty and sophistication that lives inside the introvert. Introverts don't need the world to entertain them; introverts don't need to be loud and don't need to be the center of attention. Introverts have a rich world within themselves. But if others are constantly labeling you as "anti-social" or "rude" because you are not a clown, it will distort the inner richness that only an introvert appreciates. It depends on context, but sometimes the answer is to control the term, or come up with a new term, and sometimes it is best to completely reject any term. Sometimes no label is correct.

12

Unlike religious believers, those who are nothing get to be something real, something special, and something unique. Being nothing turns out to be something, and something more interesting and charming than those caught in the tired dualism of a religious or metaphysical mentality. When you cast off religion, you can create yourself without supernatural baggage. Casting off religion is a necessary condition to creating your best self, for when you are holding on to false beliefs, your actions cannot match your beliefs. You cannot resolve the theory/practice dualism when your theory is bogus. If someone finds that a scientific theory does not work in practice, the scientific theory is refuted; it is proven bogus. If someone constructs a theory of God, and God doesn't dialogue, the theory of God is refuted; it is proven bogus. By rejecting the idea of the supernatural, we are positioned to have consistency within theory and practice. Casting off religion is not sufficient, but it is necessary to living a life of truth, to living a philosophy of practice. We see then that to say "I'm nothing" is not to say "I'm nothing." It does not mean "nothing." It might mean "I'm a philosopher."

More needs to be said, but it should be clear that we are entering the confusing and contradictory world of dialectical materialism. From a dialectical standpoint, something may turn out only to be something because it is also nothing. Religion gave birth to the idea of atheism, which in turn leads to a rejection of both. This rejection — this negation — this nothing — is something, as it is an advance beyond belief in God and atheism. In this way, then, it is not what it is (it is not nothing), even as it is what it is not (it is nothing), or perhaps it is what it is (it is nothing) only as it is becoming what it is not (as it becomes more than nothing).

13

Unlike a dialectical approach, a metaphysical approach is a straitjacket, it is reductionist. A metaphysical approach claims the world just is the way it is, and this prevalent view is captured in the popular saying "it is what it is." Both metaphysics and clichés attempt to deny history, interpretation, and contingency in favor of absolute truth, an objective world, and so-called common sense. As such, a metaphysical stance misses what is the case and what is not the case, as well as why it is or isn't the case. The metaphysical urge can be seen in the saying "it is what it is" and the saying "just sayin'." Both reify the world or the situation; through language they attempt to conceal *why* it is what it is and conceal *what* one is really saying. In other words, nothing just is what it is; the world is the way it is because we made it this way. And no one is merely "just sayin'" something; when people say something they are trying to make a point about something or point something out. To think these statements are simple unmediated truths, or merely common sense, is to adopt what György Lukács called the "contemplative attitude." The contemplative attitude is an attitude that views the world as independent of us and believes that knowledge is acquired by passive observation. The contemplative attitude is a metaphysical attitude. Just as metaphysics tries to take the human element out of the world, these sayings try to deny the human element or true meaning within the construction of each statement. This is the strategy of metaphysical and God language. This is an attitude that longs for a world outside us. This is a viewpoint that insists we are but passive observers of reality, rather than recognizing and acknowledging how we are always creating and recreating the world, and how language is active in creating meaning as opposed to simply being a sign that captures truth.

When one answers the question "are you a believer or an atheist?" with "I'm nothing," it begins to demystify bad epistemology and false metaphysics. Saying "I'm nothing" signals a dialectical and active materialist stance and implies that rejecting God and atheism is not to believe in nothing. To assert "I'm nothing" is to assert the priority of reflective action over unreflective belief, and it is to assert that even language is a material power. It is to understand that ideas have materiality, are material. Ideas only exist as part of a humanly created material world. Our ideas are materially in our books and our bodies. Ideas are linked to language, which is linked to our tongues, our ears, our brains, and to others. The idea of the supernatural arises in a material world; it is a construction of the human animal. And the human animal has a thinking brain that is active, interactive, material, physical, real, and creative. It can even create false beliefs. Sometimes we invent an idea, forget we invented it, and end up giving it a life of its own. Humans invented the idea of the supernatural. If we believe in the supernatural as some independent, non-material thing, we have a false belief. We do not have knowledge. Knowledge is constructed through material practices and is a reflective action. The supernatural, by definition, is independent of the natural and materialist world, and, as such, is outside human subjectivity. It is a term with no extension. In other words, it does not exist. The belief in the supernatural is a fragmented notion derived from certain material practices. When we forget this we outwit ourselves.

People should not be too hard on themselves if they believe in God, gods, religion, or the supernatural. We did not make these up; we did not invent them. People before us invented these ideas, and many have used them to give themselves power. It has been in the interest of many to convince us to believe. Just as we should not be too hard on ourselves for some beliefs, we also really cannot be proud of mere beliefs. People can only be proud of what they do. That's why it's amusing, and sometimes annoying, when we see believers pumping out their chests and exclaiming with such pride — We're Christians — as if this false belief is something to brag about. Sometimes they even show up at the front door to tell you about their special belief. In any case, the real good news is that we can do away with belief in the supernatural, but it will take more than non-belief; it will take philosophical action.

14

A negative belief (in the sense of negation) such as atheism cannot be a positive action, and so cannot be completely true, for truth must be proved in reality. Atheism is just a belief, an idea. It's a negative principle. A scientist can study nature, an artist can create art, but an atheist can only deny a God that doesn't exist anyway. This is why the plausibility of atheism only became viable as belief in supernatural beings became more salient. And in fact only when religion demanded acceptance, only when religious people insisted that others also be religious, did atheism come into being. As religion became totalitarian, as it moved toward monotheism, it needed a foil. In other words, the move from polytheism to monotheism played a big role here in articulating the idea of atheism. In Ancient Greece different people followed different gods, but this fact didn't mean that one also had to deny all other gods, and it didn't mean that one had to proclaim that all other religious beliefs were false and that non-belief was untrue and immoral. Atheism, in Ancient Greece, didn't necessarily mean non-belief in gods. It sometimes just meant not concerned about gods or not interested in the supernatural. Christianity, though, insisted that its metaphysical belief system was the only truth, and that all other gods and religions had to be rejected. One had to be explicitly for God or against God. Only under these dogmatic circumstances did the title of atheism become robust.

In this sense, then, Christianity gave birth to atheism, and ironically, atheism became the highest articulation of Christianity. Only atheists really take the idea of God seriously. They take it so seriously, and follow the implications of the belief so strictly, that they realize that they must reject it, for it is false. To take Christianity seriously is to see its utter irrationality, foolishness, and baseness, and once seen, to take a conscientious step and reject it, despite all of the social, cultural, and existential advantages of holding on to religion. Christianity is especially difficult to let go of since it offers a cheap and direct ticket to security, group acceptance, peace of mind, an answer to the meaning of life, an explanation of the universe, and existential security against death. The Big Book's title should be: *Answers to the Big Questions for Dummies*. This is not meant as mere insult. These types of manuals can be good and helpful. And the Bible contains some beautiful passages.

But we are dummies when it comes to metaphysical and epistemological issues. It's not our fault. It is in the interest of some not to educate us. Just look at the history of the Bible and remember it took a Protestant revolution to even get the text in the vernacular. Protestantism was a cure for some of the irrationalities and abuses of Catholicism. Today, though, one must go further. One can acknowledge that atheism is a powerful antidote against the supernatural, but once cured, we still need to live. Atheism and Christianity, because of their history, are internally intertwined. A further step, beyond both, is required. Atheists and Christians are caught in a vicious dialectic that will not end until both become uninteresting, until the notion of passively discovering Truth becomes passé, until the contemplative attitude is rejected. We will either continue to have both or we will grow up and have neither. But one cannot count on Christians to make the mature and right step, so atheists need to refuse to be foils for theists.

15

This is more complicated than it may initially seem. The old metaphysical view stresses the idea of a simple discovery and adherence to absolute truth as central. The new dialectical view implies that to overcome both God and atheism, the ability to create and a certain historical acuity are salient in consciousness. The language of interpretation and creation replaces the language of facts and discovery. And language is important. Religious language paints an antiquated and irrational picture of the world, but it has so saturated our vocabulary that it is difficult to paint the world with more beautiful colors and with better paint. Atheist discourse today is too loud and the colors are obnoxious. Atheists today resemble artists trying to paint over a canvas that already has too much old and bad paint on it, so whatever they add keeps chipping, falling off, or dulling the work. We need a new canvas but we cannot start from scratch. We have to start from our moment of history. Yet we can stretch the canvas by growing beyond medieval correspondence theory and Platonic metaphysics. One might argue that we have moved beyond these, but the binary language of theism/atheism and the reality of exploitation and alienation today refute this. The problems of philosophy must be solved in reality. The real is the rational and the rational is the real. Until we become nothing, until we have human meaning and reconciliation in our world, we will still be tribal, even in our philosophy. Philosophy becomes more than tribalism when we start to get beyond religious discourse, as we articulate a philosophy of practice that sees knowledge as a reflective action, that understands the world as our creation as much as we are its. As such, the canvas starts to come alive, as we see ourselves in the painting, as the painting, through an interactive process of creative looking and concretely acting.

To speak metaphysically, the dialectic wants to move forward, not simply move. Religion and atheism as labels are really instances of the urge to discover timeless and essential truth. But the quest for timeless and essential truth has had its day; it's time for it to retire to make room for younger, more charming quests, to make room for maturity to breathe and grow. Some ideas, like some people, hog the world. And they have center stage not because of merit or truth, but because of power. The critique of God and atheism then is a challenge to these sorts of unjustified power. So, more than dumping distracting labels such as atheism, it's important to analyze our current practices and attempt to forge new thoughtful actions. This is not the place to spell those actions out, but we can say that a dialectical approach will "naturally" challenge anything claiming to be supernatural and anything that misses our contribution to its construction. When we accept the notion of something or someone outside (and above) us, we are also implicitly legitimating practices that are alienating and exploitative, and we do so in the name of a fiction. Against this, a dialectical approach can challenge anything or anyone trying to lord over us. As such, a dialectical approach can challenge capitalist and state institutions when they perpetuate the contemplative attitude. A dialectical approach can challenge, through its internal logic, through dialogue, undemocratic institutions. An approach with no interest in trying to transcend us only works when it is dialogic. We can all speak, so the dialectic is internally suited to be democratic. Non-democratic dialogue is not justified when our obligations are only to each other. Without democracy, some people will feel inadequate and will be treated inadequately; some people will abuse their power; and certain individuals will be de-centered, while others will be too centered. Under these conditions the urge to look to another realm to escape, to transcend, will reappear. Those without power will look for an outside to appease themselves, while those with power will rationalize their power using the supernatural; so everyone needs equal power. No one should be marginalized.

But one must be careful here, for there will be blowback. Those who have social and political power will feel threatened, and those who are invested in religious ideology will not be amused. They will feel personally and materially attacked, and they will try to convince you, or force you, to get back in line. They will even accuse you of being unethical because of your democratic sensibilities and your sense of obligation to other dialogue partners. Don't believe them, don't fall for their manipulation; prove them wrong through your philosophical actions. We can form ourselves and create human meaning and recognize that that's meaning enough. What are you, Christians or atheists? *We're nothing, and that's saying a lot. It's enough to want to form ourselves and make ourselves and those who matter proud.*

16

As we have seen, the idea here is that if the God/atheism binary is problematic, if it's a type of codependency, then the death of God might also entail the death of atheism. When your project dissolves away or becomes unimportant, then perhaps your nemesis also dissolves away or becomes unimportant. But as Nietzsche said, perhaps we have come too early, for most people don't see this or won't admit it. We do see it sometimes. Look at sports. When athletes retire, they often become friends with those whom they battled against and perhaps couldn't defeat while playing. When people retire, you cannot really be against them anymore, for they are no longer there to defeat. When something dies, you cannot be against it anymore, for it doesn't exist in order to challenge. At most you can look back and understand the fight, or analyze and critique it; but you don't live in real opposition to it any more. You must move on. If one realizes there is no God, can one really spend one's life opposing God? You don't want to end up like Don Quixote. Rather than fighting windmills, rather than living for, or dwelling on, anachronistic beliefs, the good warrior comes back to reality and concentrates on fulfilling obligations to real people and real things. The death of God implies the death of atheism, as the death of Truth implies the death of relativism. In the former case we transcend into ourselves and the recognition that God was always a projection from us. In the latter case we recognize that we are responsible for making the world true. The world only falls into relativism or nihilism if we let it, if we choose it. In this way we can say that if you need a God, Truth, or an unquestioned authority above you to do the right thing, then you may also need a bed time.

17

Going through the process of seeing God/atheism as two sides of the same coin, a coin we created and could discard, can move us toward a new process, a process that rejects the binary, that rejects the coin itself. Still, we can embrace those aspects of both that have gotten us as far as they have. We can be honest about the ways they have misguided us. And we can look back and face our history as a living history, one whose obligations are ultimately only to other people. The French gave up the franc, but it doesn't mean that they abandoned their past or that their past was one big mistake. Rather, that currency is something to remember, and in dark times (when the euro is weak), it is something that provokes an urge to go back. But the franc is done; in reality it is only a part of French history now. The euro is the living currency, necessary for the French to make their way in the world today. And although the franc had some advantages over the euro, one should not forget the two world wars and the ease with which the Germans saw themselves as separate from the French. With the euro that alienation, we trust, is not so easy, either intellectually or materially, to achieve. The euro offers deeper opportunities to expand our common humanity. Still, the euro brings with it its own problems, just as no one is suggesting that transcending God/no-God is a panacea. But with this new perspective we have a new process, one that stops trying to discover something outside us, stops trying to appeal to or fight against some abstract authority lurking over human beings. This is dialectical philosophy. Philosophy is a reflective and critical activity that interacts with the human world and promotes active responsibility to each other, our institutions, and the world. To deny this is to deny love of wisdom.

18

Linguistically, philosophy means love of wisdom. Philosophy, from the Latin *philosophia*, breaks into *philos* and *sophia*. *Philos*, love, is love as one loves a friend; *sophia* is wisdom. The philosopher loves wisdom and wants more of it. It is not a mere belief; it is a way of being-in-the-world. It is an attitude and relationship to the world, one that strives for something more. And to love wisdom is not necessarily to possess wisdom. You may love someone or something but not *have* that someone or completely *understand* the object of desire. Love of wisdom then has a dialectical modesty rooted within it. A rooting in desire, love, friendship, meaning, and reconciliation that is not about ordinary belief; rather, it is more like a quest that searches for something higher, and perhaps something lower. It may seem clear that loving wisdom is a higher sort of quest, but how can it be lower? Well, loving something but not possessing it, loving it without really knowing it can be dangerous. If someone loves you but doesn't know you, are you comfortable with that? Is it something higher or is that someone a stalker? Philosophy is as dirty a business as any. It can take one to the highest highs and lowest lows, so you'd better get ready. And in fact you'd better come ready, for that way you don't have to get ready. If you have to get ready, it's already too late. Just ask King Lear.

With King Lear, it was too late because he was too old. There's a reason Socrates talked to the youth. Philosophy stresses the need to become wise before becoming old. We want to know that we are loved because of who we are and not because of what we represent. Do you love something because it's actually good and worth loving, or is it because it's popular and merely exciting? Do you just love someone because of his position and power, because he is the King? (And let's hope he's not the real estate king; that's just pathetic.) Or are these things part of what the thing is? Can we separate Lear from the fact that he is the King, or the individual from the real estate agent? Can we separate ourselves from what we represent, from what we believe, from what we do, from what we desire?

The *philos* side of philosophy is complicated and confusing, but so is the *sophia* side. Really, what is wisdom? It is clearly somewhat different than knowledge; it implies an interest in "bigger and higher" things. From the start it was connected to activity and the art of living. It stresses unity and harmony involving not mind/body dualism, but intersubjectivity, dialogue, and practice. As living, physical agents we seek wisdom greater than any abstract theory or solipsistic self could capture. Only a real, practical, communicative, and active materialism is worthy of the name *sophia*. We are rich creatures with an array of material aspects within us — it's all that's in us. We are bundles of flesh, bones, blood, neurons, brainpower, desires, thoughts, feelings, and so on, that are salt of the earth, so to speak. Look everywhere and you see us as we put ourselves into everything. As our eyes look up into the sky, we take in the world and form it. There is no completely separating it out from us, for as we experience it we help make it what it is at that moment. We are east, west, north, and south. Our self-creating, materialist bodies and conscious minds, in dialogue and through practice with others, are a geography which creates geography, while at the same time the world is creating us.

19

Today we might say the origin of Western Philosophy has an Eastern flair to it. Bruce Lee grasped the true origin of philosophy; he was a philosophy major. He understood the hopelessly intertwined nature of what we sometimes simplify and call "mind and body." He actualized this by inventing a new style of martial arts. Jeet Kune Do blends all the styles of fighting into a harmonious and living entity. The style was not dogmatic or arrogant. Like Socrates, he always stayed a student even as he taught the rest of us. He communicated his living philosophy through action and dialogue.

Bruce Lee's version of the Tea Cup story is relevant and moving for many. It involves a student coming to study with a master and the student is excited, can't stop talking, etc. The master is calm and quiet as he prepares the tea. He slowly begins to pour the tea as the student keeps talking: about himself, what he has done, and what he wants to do. The master continues to look at the student and continues to pour the tea, even as it is full, even as it spills over the sides of the cup. Finally, the student yells, "Stop pouring, my cup is full!" and the master says, "Yes, the cup is full, as your mind is full"; and he takes the cup and throws out all the tea, as he says, "You must empty your mind just as I emptied the cup, if you want to learn." Sometimes it is best to metaphorically throw out everything we are holding on to, even as we know this is impossible. Try to throw out God and atheism, even if just for a day. Philosophy teaches us to empty our cups, to stop fetishizing beliefs, and to start acting in ways to make ourselves and those who matter proud.

Throwing out one's beliefs, even just for a day, is difficult. But it's not completely impossible. We can try on different masks, play games, and challenge each other and ourselves. Humans are amazing. Still, some, even today, think it would be difficult to be an atheist. Whether it is the head of Duck Dynasty or Calvin, some think it's impossible not to believe in God. But we lose gods all the time. And most of the time the notion of God is far from our minds. Most things humans once thought of as linked to the supernatural are not thought of that way anymore. We don't turn to the gods to understand lightning, a bad crop, or flooding anymore. Most of our world, in fact almost all of it, for almost all of us, is understood through a secular lens. Think of the thousands of little things we do every day, and think about how de-centered they are from religion: getting our coffee, going to work and school, reading, watching the news, playing with our kids, paying bills, watching the game, most of the time we spend in church, hiking, shopping, driving, texting, internet surfing, swimming and surfing, and so on. We don't need any conception of the supernatural to go about our business. And when we do bring in the supernatural or posit a supernatural being, it's usually just an add-on. We can recognize this when we acknowledge that we stop believing, or change what things mean for us, or change our definitions of things all the time. Just think for a second about what God meant for and to you a year ago, five years ago, ten years ago etc. It's not the same. You are not the same. Religion is a fluctuating thing and a contingent thing — unlike Rambo, it's expendable.

20

Religion was invented out of fear. Yet today many people turn to religion not simply because of fear, but because it helps them experience love. The modern world can be a cold place and religion sometimes fills a void in people's lives. But, when possible, one should be aware of the origin of one's belief as well as its history, especially when that history is ambiguous to say the least. Religion, from the start, has been used to manipulate, oppress, and exclude people. Your practice of religion may not include these features, but these features are embedded into our world and supported by the foundations, both intellectually and materially, of religion. From laws to institutions, to groups, to individual beliefs, the regressive aspects of religion saturate our world. You might not consciously be religious out of fear and power, but the meaning of religion is hopelessly intertwined with fear and domination. Exhibit A: ISIS. It's similar to the debate over the Confederate flag. I'm sure some people connect to the flag in purely innocuous ways. Perhaps it makes them feel proud of their tradition, and their culture, and it gives them a feeling of love. But that's not the meaning of the Confederate flag. We cannot neatly separate out what it means to individuals from the actual history of the flag. It is an ugly racist history, and the Confederate flag is ineluctably symbolic of that history. What it means for one person's personal belief, a person's identity, is really beside the point. We are social constructions, not merely self constructions. The beliefs and practices we engage in carry meaning that transcends us. To see the Confederate flag as innocuous is to be willfully ignorant. And to see religion as innocuous is to be willfully ignorant. There are better, more mature ways, of dealing with fear and of expressing and experiencing love.

21

Still, today, too many people tend to go quickly to the supernatural when they are afraid and when things seem unexplainable. Philosophy, though, did not originate from the cry of terror as did religion. Philosophy came later, and its origins developed from lucky individuals who had leisure and were seeking for more out of life than survival. It originated from love and curiosity. Western philosophy began with a puzzle, an anomaly. Thales, perhaps the first philosopher, or proto-philosopher, saw — like those around him — that the Nile River was acting counter-intuitively and that needed to be explained. Flooding when it's hot, and drying up when cold, is not the usual pattern. When life is going according to plan, when you are in the swim, you are less likely to stop and reflect. There's no social or natural necessity to question the world or one's life. But when things are off, like a river behaving strangely, or when someone dumps you, or you lose your job, or perhaps you get seriously ill, deeper reflection might occur. Rather than jumping to myth, philosophy teaches us to use reason and experience, and to reflect and act.

Thales didn't rush in to answer the puzzle with another supernatural explanation. For Thales, the supernatural explanations just weren't cutting it. Thales tried to explain the fact that the river flooded, despite the lack of rain and the dryness, by positing a natural theory and by doing empirical research. He wanted to understand and test his ideas. He thought the winds might be causing the flooding. Not correct, but it got him closer to the truth. Apparently the water was coming from further south in Africa, upstream, where there wasn't lack of rain and it wasn't dry. Thales's natural explanations contrasted with the supernatural ones surrounding him in his day. His courage motivated the dialectic, and pushed the cry of terror, emanating from supernatural explanations, out of the human mind. Reason and the senses, rationalism and empiricism take over, and we are better off for it.

22

Still, it can be dangerous to challenge supernatural explanations, but if your new explanation or new behavior works, others will tend to listen or follow. In this way, fine tuning one's reason is easier to do when dealing with nature. It's smart to stay away from the sexy stuff at first. Religious, political, or existential debates carry lots of emotional baggage, so jumping into them requires particular tact and sensitivity. But even questions of science need to be grounded and mediated through philosophy; otherwise science's ideology, the desires and interests behind it, will be forgotten or ignored. Why did Thales need to give a scientific explanation? The story most philosophers tell, starting with Aristotle through today, is that Thales wanted to prove that philosophy was a worthwhile activity, that reason and observation is the human route to truth. It's a noble story and partly true. Thales was correct that supernatural explanations are inadequate, and Thales was trying to legitimate his scientific practices. Yet he was also a businessman and heavily involved with politics, and he used his mathematical and scientific skill for business success and political advantage. In this way science is no different from religion. Under certain social conditions both can be used in the service of business and politics, and without critical reflection, both can legitimate the bad, the false, and the ugly.

This is why Socrates is so important. Socrates understood that scientific questions are, at best, merely a means to help one live a successful human life. Science gives explanations, and these explanations carry not just scientific facts within them but also hidden meaning and value. Philosophy is needed to give form to the object or event—form so that, with the scientific understanding of the object or the event, individuals can still make sense of their lives and connect this sense to others and to the world. Further, the "facts" of science need to be demystified so we remember that they are really interpretations. Any so-called facts come to be understood, and in fact created, through human history. They carry our language, perspectives, needs, and interests within them. They are not clean or outside us. We actively contribute to their existence and meaning. They are a power. Powerful interpretations have two important features. First they help promote understanding. They help us make sense of ourselves, of who we are and what we want to become. They tap into our traits, characteristics, and values; they are intrinsically worthwhile. Second, powerful interpretations are pragmatic. They help us get better at our practices, and our activities, and perhaps aid us in survival. They have instrumental value.

This is the materialist secret hiding within belief in God and rejection of God. Together, theism and atheism form a Blood Moon, an eclipse blocking out the sun, blocking philosophy as reflective action. The redness betrays the bloody past of religion, while it also foreshadows the color of the utopian future. As ideological forms they reflect and rationalize our world. Yet they are not the true source of light and they are not eternal. An eclipse will not sustain but can and will reoccur. Ideological beliefs reoccur because they offer seductive and powerful interpretations that capture important aspects of our humanity, yet often in childish forms. With each reoccurrence, new opportunities for living and new interpretations present themselves. We must learn to perceive with more humanity, for at some point we won't get another chance for maturity.

Religion, and especially monotheistic versions such as Christianity, harbors the intrinsic within their forms. Religion has been a major player in holding on to our quest for the intrinsically good, for positing final ends, but it is time to relinquish this role that no longer suits it. It has been an important home of virtue, character, and authentic traits, but has refused to actualize them. The holy already feel special, so they have no motivation to grow or make the world better. Instead of seriously questioning things, they naively walk around saying things such as "I'm blessed." Instead of reading books like *Why Good People Do Bad Things* (Hollis, not Ford), they read *Why Bad Things Happen to Good People*, so they never grow. Further, some of our essential human traits so thoroughly scare the holy that they try to purge themselves and the world of them without understanding them, and the repression creates monsters. Anyone forced to attend Catholic school will understand this.

Like religion, atheism has a sublime yet distorting secret. While it pitches itself as a belief holding up truth, it is, on a deeper level, really an angle for cultivating instrumental good. Atheism pushes back against religious fear and superstition, and prompts us to seize this world and to practically and pragmatically push into the future. Still, it has difficulty positing final ends and creating substantial meaning. It relies on religion as much as religion relies on the profane. Tangled with religion, it has never been able to displace it and never will. Religion and atheism together hold within them sublime secrets for living, but they mystify and reify the secrets into impotent beliefs and regressive action. We can though, through will and consciousness, demystify these ideas, and grasp the human practices that were always already there creating them, and in doing so we unlock the key to completing the quest to make ourselves and those who matter proud.

23

Still, today though, this view sounds naïve. We are modern, and ancient religions and reactionary beliefs have had to give way to the new God: science. Of course science is vitally important, but there was a good reason Socrates choose philosophy over science. Science and technology can help us cultivate our instrumental side by making our lives easier, but they cannot directly transform the meaning and value our lives have. Science and technology stem from human interest and human need, not the other way around. They are, at best, mere aids to living the good life; they do not teach us the good life. As such they can be used ideologically, strategically, and even for evil, as easily as they can be used to improve human lives. They can often be a poor substitute for understanding. Online college classes that emphasize standardization, assessment, outputs, and profits are proof enough of this.

We are constantly, and often unconsciously, creating and recreating the meaning and value of science and technology, but we need to do so with more critical reflection and social planning, not through market forces. If we allow science and technology to float above us, or trust in their paternalism, then we reify them and are primed for ideological manipulation. Do you really think that even good companies such as Google are first and foremost interested in making your life better? If making the human condition better were the driving force behind our new techie elites, then we would see them arguing for worker control of the means of production and democratic control of the consumption realm. Science and technology are great, but the point is we must never forget that science and technology are especially susceptible (because of their impressive instrumental success) of becoming slaves to economic interests, and in turn destroying the intrinsic good. Their effect, too often, is to distract us from creating meaningful and valuable lives.

24

The need to integrate science and technology rationally into our lives, rather than being determined by market forces, is more pressing than ever. We all feel this. Films such as *Ex Machina* and *Her* warn us of the dystopian future that is actually already upon us. Humanity has been dreaming about the virtual world and the age of robots for a long time. We can view the cartoon television show *The Jetsons* today and laugh at our naivety in thinking about the future, and at the same time, it can send chills down our spines to realize how off our predictions of the future have been. Do we want robots; do we want to become robots? In *Ex Machina* we see the dream of the first woman, of Eve, and we see the *femme fatale* that is still a bogeyman in patriarchal society. In patriarchal society even the bogeyman is a woman. And as woman, the machine is not quite human. Computer technology runs at a different pace than the human mind. The human mind is slow and plotting, while computer technology is merely a theory that runs incredibly fast and without thought. Is the patriarchal assumption that women are simply intuitive, hopelessly irrational, and more "naturally" driven being sublimated into our notions of a dystopian future? Is the current fad with the first human, the race to find our nearest relatives, deeply connected to our fears about the technological future? From the Eve myth to Ava, the fear of the woman who is tricking the man, making him a cuckold, and doing it all on instinct, while she wields her apple or knife, moves seamlessly and effortlessly from *Genesis* through *Fatal Attraction* to *Ex Machina*.

25

There is a part of us that dreams of transcending our contingency and fallibility through science and technology, from slowness to pre-reflective processing, or from philosophy to machine. It's an attempt to escape into a new metaphysics, structurally the same as a religious type of letting go. Just as it is to give up one's human form in the name of spirituality, or for God, it is dangerous to let go of slowness and human depth in the name of technological progress. As Kundera warns us in his sublime novel *Slowness*: "Why has the pleasure of slowness disappeared...In our world, indolence has turned into having nothing to do, which is a completely different thing: a person with nothing to do is frustrated, bored, is constantly searching for the activity he lacks."[1] Against sublime slowness, our world celebrates nonstop activity, such as constantly checking one's cell phone, saying "I'm so busy" with pride. It is a flight from the self, a death wish determined to defeat the existential anxiety of being human. And it could happen and is happening. With constant texting, online and mall shopping, internet surfing, radio and commercial music blaring, television binging, and tweeting or Facebooking every stupid moment, the ability for reflection and slowness is thwarted. Technology need not demand lack of reflection, but a commodified technology banks on it. As more and more of our world becomes subject to abstraction, subject to mathematical logic, we will see this quantitative shift transform, in quasi-Hegelian fashion, into a qualitative difference. It's only quasi-Hegelian because the transformation will not be an evolution or progression. It will be a qualitative change back to a time before consciousness; it will be robots without thought, as we will come full circle, back to the missing link, the forgotten species, back to before Lucy.

26

That's why philosophy must be careful not to fall victim to the search for method. If 20th-century analytic philosophy has taught us anything, it is that the search for method is a fool's errand. Method will destroy individuality and thinking. It will destroy philosophy. Rejecting method though is not to reject form. There is no Form, only many forms suitable for different things, and each of them only emerges through content. Rather than searching for God or for a method, both of which are attempts to bypass thought, the form suggested here rejects the notion of something outside of us. Rather this form sees the world as only emerging as form emerges, and it views form as only forming through the world, not prior to it. In this way it makes more sense to think of form in terms of simply trying to form ourselves and see

---

1 Kundera, *Slowness* 3.

ourselves in all that we take as outside us. For something to be intelligible to us, to even perceive it, we must interpret it. In this way the world is always already mediated by interpretation, and is in this sense our creation. Nothing is known without a knower, and we are the knowers. As knowers, we must also know that we carry ourselves into whatever we encounter. In this way the world is always already linked to us.

We must also guard against getting stuck in individualism or atomism, though. Our minds (that are also our bodies) are part of the ever-evolving world, and content and form start from the outside. When the mind gets constructed, gets "filled" (like in the Tea Cup story), this filling comes from the outside. Even language comes from outside the individual. We are a historical and social construction, not a self-construction. Still, when the cup starts to fill, it merges, mind and body, as the subject becomes a force unto itself, and becomes more and more capable of forming itself and choosing content through reflective action. But there is never a "one" when it comes to the self. The self is a wonderland: complex, deep, and yes, commodified. It is always in the world as the world is in it. To quote that sentimental 80s song: "We are the World." The world exists through us as much as we exist through the world, and it's all related, in a million little scattered pieces which come together and become something new when we speak, think, act, and even sing. Without us there is no forming even a sentimental 80s song; without us there is no forming our world.

27

These ideas on form relate to Lukács's *Soul and Form*. In *Soul and Form* Lukács, following Kassner, contrasts two types[1]: the creative artist and the critic, or, put differently, the poet and the Platonist. What interests Kassner and Lukács is how the former feels full while the latter has a sense of longing. The poet is drenched in verse and this verse reflects a poet's being. The Platonist finds grounding in prose and directly tries to unite with the universal. The answer to the dialectic between the poet and the Platonist is not a simple counterbalance of the two. Like the dialectic between theism and atheism, the answer is not agnosticism. Each of these only ends in an empty mediocrity. A dialectical approach rejects counterbalance for something more, dare one say — evolutionary. Yet this evolution is peculiar in that it is an active and conscious transformation into something else, perhaps something higher, but it evolves by changing form rather than simply because of environment and content.

Actually it's more complicated than this. According to Lukács one senses that a new form is needed for expression, so content and environment does

1 See Lukács, *Soul and Form*, Chapter 2.

prompt a change in form, while at the same time form is changing before new content or the environment directly asks it to. And this change can happen because it's driven by one's internal process, mediated with the external. To use Lukács's metaphor, the poet and the Platonist keep writing although the form and style of each writer might change. Writing is the condition for any written form, and what is written articulates the mediation between the internal and external. It requires mind and body, thought and hand, pen and paper, earth and trees, all interacting through a subject and between subjects. The mediation creates unity within and through the unfolding of the text. It is a human labor requiring subjectivity and objectivity. The subject, through thoughtful action, drives the writing and creates the object. The object only exists, in that form, through and because of the subject. The form of writing doesn't exist without a writer. All writing has something of the writer in it, and all objects in our world have something of human subjectivity in them. Human subjectivity is the condition for any knowledge, and what is known epistemologically, like form molding content, ontologically brings our world into being, although the potential content of the world was always there. Our world is always connected to human subjectivity. Through dialogue, through the articulation and testing of truth claims, that is to say through philosophical action, we create knowledge and the world. Subjectivity always already creates, as it is alive, and takes in the world and puts itself into the world through constant interaction and mediation. From our breath to our movements to our thoughts, it never stops, and we never separate from the world or it from us. Sometimes the connection takes the form of literally transforming the world or ourselves. We paint something or we get a tattoo, we build cities or muscle, we grow food or eat something, we read or we write. And sometimes the link is more subtle as we "merely" think about the world, and contemplate ourselves and objects in our world. And sometimes we don't need to write our thoughts down, but just keep them in us. In this way our world and all objects in it always contain the subjective, always contain us.

28

One might say that still the world must exist regardless of us, and we might counter that we can dream and create existence beyond the given world, too. And the former claim is only true in thought or in theory, since we are here, while the latter is true in reality, since we have transformed the world in thought and in practice. In this sense human life is the necessary condition for our world. Without our dialogue, without our truth claims, both of which come out of our material practices, there is no knowledge and there is not this world. This world is the world, the only world. It is us and we are it. Going back to Lukács's analogy, then, as we "write" the world we create it and make it intelligible. It never ends so long as there are subjects to write and read. In this way, then, we can never give up writing.

Writing and reading, speaking and listening, making truth claims and questioning truth claims, are things only humans do. Dialogue is from us and between us. No gods, no other part of nature or the world, speak as we do. And it is only because of dialogue and through dialogue that we can create normativity, meaning, and value. Normativity, meaning, and value have a human form. If they exist at all it is because of us, and it is through our dialogue that they come into being. Justifying them is to act; it is to test them with others in dialogue. In this way our world stays within the human. The human form cannot be transcended. When we forget this we reify ourselves and our world.

29

Neither the poet nor the Platonist can transcend the human form. They never give up the form of writing, so to speak, but the writing changes and may become something new as it interacts with life. In life we keep living; we don't give up living in order to live something new and better. In this way then evolution or transcendence is not transcendence away and above writing or life; rather, it is through writing and through living. Staying within the discursive act, the reflective act, by going deeper through form, allows the dialectical artist to unify the poetic and the Platonic elements. On can therefore say form combines unity and multiplicity. This may sound mysterious, but it really is not. Great writers have always created unique and new forms. In terms of philosophers we see this play out in masters as diverse as Plato and Marx. Plato was not a Platonist and Marx was not a Marxist. Both were dialectical artists who took their poetic and Platonic parts and created transcendent works of art. Both created in ways that those before them could not. And both could not be directly imitated. In the case of Marx, unlike many of his followers, he was not merely fixated on discovering economic laws, just as Plato, unlike his acolytes, was not so straightforwardly committed to the Forms. Both show us ways of living essentially different human lives, even as they remain philosophers. This is what is meant by human life creating the world. There is nothing supernatural or superhuman; there is no transcendence without us or beyond us. What lies beyond us would not be our world, and it would not and could not exist with us. Because of us the world is not unintelligible; without us it is not intelligible.

What Lukács calls the poetic and Platonic types, we see in the atheist and Christian types on college campuses today. Born into this dualistic world, young students cannot help but get caught up in one or the other side of the dialectic. We see young poets who drift through college letting the winds blow them from class to class, from idea to idea, from ideology to ideology. They take in a little of everything but cannot unify it to build their lives. Our world makes it difficult to actualize their poetic dreams, or even to give them coherent form, let alone materialize them. On the other side we also see the intelligent but too religious students. Their dreams are clear but these dreams are not really their dreams. Their minds have been preloaded with someone else's worn out belief system. They have been spooked by their ignorant elders, in a type of reverse and perverse Socratic teaching, so they go through college but never open themselves to knowledge and wisdom. When young, an individual has a unique opportunity in that, if unformed enough, and willing enough, the being-of-the-world (which is actually also a becoming) will reveal itself and show the beauty that is only possible when certain aspects of the world combine with a young mind. For, if fortunate, a young consciousness is empty enough and receptive enough to take in the good that our world has to offer. Only within this "potential philosopher" can a certain type of creative beauty take root and grow. The tragedy of our time is that too many with potential get filled with infantile–capitalist garbage or unimaginative–religious laws. It creates an immaturity not ready to blossom into creative beauty, but instead takes the poetic part and uses it to manufacture an immaturity that doesn't want to grow up; and it takes the Platonic part and ensures it cannot bravely confront contingencies. The former creates a playful but rudderless student while the latter makes for a reliable but weary one. Both suffer the danger of ending in a type of inward suicide (perhaps the former results in a PC liberal and the latter becomes an unctuous Republican). Yet it doesn't have to be this way. Both those who come to college corrupted and those who are rudderless may transcend their fate if they are lucky enough to encounter that one voice that speaks to them and unlocks an edifying practice in them. And that one voice could be anyone from Socrates to Sartre. That is the beauty of college. There is a chance to awaken truth in both types. College is subversive and outlaw with the potential to transcend the one-sidedness of the poet or the Platonist. But not directly. Professors who are explicitly political are the worst. Teaching one's discipline honestly and deeply is the road to creating beautiful individuals. Richard Rorty's phrase "take care of freedom and truth will take care of itself"[1] captures this.

31

We live in a time where thought (I'm using the word loosely) is the result of a direct pipeline from the base. In the age of the internet, the corporate age, the time of the Nation State, we are tubes wrapped in deadening insulation. This insulation creates an echo chamber blocking out coherent sounds and beautiful music. We are fed the sound bites echoing the masters' voices, voices that are saturated with the ruling class interests. From *Bose* to *Beats* shouting straight into mind the world of amusements distract us from our wasteful society. In an act of malevolent distraction, it is easy for ideological interests to echo throughout the lifeworld at a pitch that the human ear cannot grasp. Virtual words are power. The economic players have control of discourse and the social discourse runs through us like oil in the machine. We are no longer cogs in the machine, rather we are pipes — filled with commodified memes — transporting the falseness that is our world. As Amélie Nothomb puts it so beautifully in *The Character of Rain*: humans as pipes "are singular combinations of fullness and emptiness; they are hollow substance, a something that contains nothing. Tubes can be flexible, but it renders them no less mysterious."[2] She further captures, in Freudian fashion, our modern way of being-in-the-world, and the infantile feeling of being God in one's solipsistic, yet virtual and consuming world: "GOD'S SOLE PREOCCUPATIONS were ingestion, digestion, and, as a direct result, excretion. These vegetative activities took place without God's even being aware of them. Nourishment, always the same, wasn't exciting enough to take much note of. God simply opened all the appropriate orifices for it to pass in, and through, and out."

Even so we are not completely hopeless, as we are still the ones creating and recreating it all. We simply need to gain self-reflection and adopt different practices. We need to destroy the poison in the pipes — the reified aspects of ourselves — and the structures feeding them. This begins though by slowing the oil and reflecting on our reified essence through a process of filtering out the dirt. We must reflect on where to take our freedom, rather than simply blow everything up. The poet cannot completely eclipse the Platonist unless the poet creates a better foundation; the Platonist can't just slip into nihilism when the Forms dissolve into relativity. Even a false universal can provide guidance, as adolescent folly can provoke inspiration. Perhaps we begin by

---

1 See Richard Rorty's *Take Care of Freedom and Truth Will Take Care of Itself.*
2 All my quotations in this section from Amélie Nothomb are from her novel *The Character of Rain*, 2–3.

weaning ourselves from overseas oil, as well as the oil drum of the stupid culture industry, and the unctuous beat of contemporary religion. The false dialectic — the bankrupt language of Capitalism and God — the reified discourse of atheism and theism — is not just ideological, it is alienating and exploitative. It is the language of a class society and a power that materially reproduces our class society. It is the one-sided and corrupted language of an older cynical poet and a worn out dogmatic Platonist trying to destroy each other in an act of totalitarian assertion, instead of confronting their squandered youth. This divisive totalitarian urge is in us as deeply as the urge to create and unite — Thanatos and Eros — at war within us, seemingly endlessly, like the gods of Manicheanism. We must defeat the false dialectic through a reflective act of self-recognition that carries our beauty into being.

32

The phenomenon of total reification, to adopt Lukács's terminology, is more sinister than the old factory exploitation. With the old factory exploitation one could gain some distance when not at work. But today the whole world is a factory. Adorno's line about Marx wanting to turn the whole world into a workhouse has been horribly accomplished; but in a darker way than either Marx or Adorno ever could have envisioned. The world is a structural workhouse from factory to Facebook. Capitalism is still the power that must be confronted, but this power speaks through God-speak and immature irony. God-speak, with its Siamese twin sister immature irony, are integrated into the forces and relations of production, even as they seem to live above in the superstructure. The superstructure is just a vacation home where they show off. Their real dwelling is in a much deeper place. We get a glimpse of this place in the most seemingly innocuous places. Going through In-N-Out Burger, one feeds the profane modern stomach, and with the bible verses hidden under the Coke cup, the metaphysical soul gets quenched. Culture is all about some "God" or the denial of some "God." In either case it trickles down to feed the base that created it.

Yet we miss much because we have a fetish for the State. Obama and Clinton and Trump dominate. In reality the state is just a middle man. It settles in between the base and superstructure such that we see political God-speak and immature irony both working on the behalf of, and at the behest of, the ruling class. In the internet age the commodification of discourse is complete. Like water through pipes it runs from the base, through the state, into the superstructure and endlessly repeats in a vulgarized Nietzschean eternal recurrence until the water is undrinkable. Yet no one notices since one must be human, or at least vegetable, in order to need water. Virtual being and metal heads only short circuit or rust when wet. But true metal heads, like Socrates, are misunderstood and stereotyped. Those on the outside miss what is really going on; they miss the possibility for an aesthetic education, sensitive to the harmony and disharmony, the civilizing and the barbaric, the individual and the group. To move beyond passively gazing up at the beauty of the Blood Moon, that today is Christianity and atheism, we will first turn to the metal head of the ancient world, to Socrates (gold, of course), all the while making sure the sublime eclipse is fleeting, until only the active light of philosophy remains.

CHAPTER 2. SOCRATES'S STORY

1

Introduction to philosophy courses often begin with Plato. Sometimes students have to read a series of early Socratic dialogues including *Euthyphro*, *Apology*, *Crito*, and the death scene from the *Phaedo*. It's a good selection of dialogues to begin one's philosophical education; an education that usually only lasts a semester. An introduction to philosophy course is also likely to be an exit from philosophy, as students move on to different subjects, often running away from the strange and foreign philosophical experience. Socrates may be presented as a coherent character so that students have a story to better help grasp the concepts as well as remember him. Reading these early dialogues, that give a somewhat fictionalized account of his final days, constructs Socrates as a memorable character. Reading the dialogues together, as one text, constructs Socrates as a story; it's a fiction, but an interesting and useful one. The idea of one's life as a story is popular right now and has been for a while. Perhaps too popular. There are advantages and disadvantages to this metaphor, but one should always remember, it is just a metaphor. A life is not a story. Rather, our lives are lived moment by moment, and are more similar to a series of photographs, and fleeting memories, that are both real and unreal. We can weave them together in various patterns and arrange these snapshots in such a way that it feels as if our lives have a narrative structure. Despite this feeling, we don't want to succumb to bad faith, especially when reading Socrates, the guy who said — know thyself.

2

The first dialogue, *Euthyphro*, displays Plato's brilliance as a dialectical writer. This work highlights both his desire for absolutes, his Platonism, and at the same time, our desire for theatre and spectacle. The drama is as central to understanding the text as the philosophical arguments are. The dialogue starts with Socrates at the courthouse. He's only there because he needs to read the affidavit against him, so he can know what he is being sued for, what the charges against him are. But, of course, there will be some people just hanging out, trying to catch the gossip. It is surprising to see Socrates at the courthouse, for he is known not to care about gossip. Also, it's probably surprising that he is being sued. He is old and doesn't bother people who don't bother him. The ancient courthouse must have been lively, while today there're much easier ways to catch the gossip. When I was a kid you could turn on the local radio station on Monday morning to find out who got arrested over the weekend. Today you just need to open your computer or check your phone. Gossip comes to us, today. We don't have to seek it out; it seeks us out. In the checkout aisle, at the gas pump, in the waiting room, on the local news or TMZ, outside the courthouse, and so on, we are exposed 24/7 to gossip, and we do seem to enjoy it. We know we are all a bit naughty and nice, and this fact must be accounted for, celebrated, condemned, and fed. The media lives on hope and fear, and gossip is a main dish. The story of Socrates speaks to us, not just because he offered insight into the big questions but because he was a subject of gossip, rumors, and was even parodied in a popular play of the day (*The Clouds*). Bigger than all these other S's — O. J. Simpson, M. Steward, Saddam Hussein, Scott Peterson, Jeffrey Skilling — Socrates's drama stands out. If suing Socrates can be a thing, then no one is safe.

3

Socrates is being accused of three things. He is charged with corrupting the youth, not believing in the gods of the state, and in having his own divinities. The latter two charges basically amount to a claim of impiety. Words like piety and impiety are not thrown around too much today. Even similar words such as righteousness and ungodliness don't come up much. But we get the general idea. Socrates is thought not to be worshipping the right gods, or not to be worshipping in the right sort of way, if at all. But apparently it is Socrates's lucky day, for he runs into a man who claims to be holy and to understand what it means to be pious. This man, Euthyphro, when hearing about the charges against Socrates, claims to be able to help. Men like Euthyphro, the do-gooders, think of themselves as good citizens and they see their religion as connected to their sense of citizenship. Euthyphro believes he understands the gods and acts in accordance with their norms. From the start we can tell that Euthyphro is a buffoon. But then, with Plato, it's never quite that simple because, despite himself, Euthyphro is on to something radical and perhaps deeply ethical. Euthyphro is speaking for someone without voice.

Euthyphro is doing something that would have been extremely rare at his time and is still unusual today. He is suing his father. Not only is he suing his father but he is accusing his father of murder. It's especially interesting because, first, his father didn't literally kill anyone, and second, the person who is dead is a slave. What exactly happened? Well, two slaves got into a fight and one killed the other. The father had the guilty slave bound and thrown into a ditch for the authorities to pick up. But before anyone came to retrieve the guilty slave, he died in the ditch. Euthyphro holds his father responsible for the death of this slave and he wants the court to punish him. Legally it was not Euthyphro's place to see that his father was punished. That would be the job of the slave's family. We don't know why they were not involved. Perhaps he had no family. Today we might commend Euthyphro for giving voice to the dead slave. He is attempting to do justice for the dead slave. It is a bit surprising that Socrates does not commend Euthyphro. In fact Socrates is only interested in Euthyphro's claim to understand piety and in Euthyphro's reasoning concerning piety. But as a philosopher, shouldn't Socrates be concerned with justice for the slave, regardless of whether Euthyphro was following the legal precedent? Shouldn't Socrates applaud Euthyphro? Perhaps; and today most of us at least see that Euthyphro has a point. You just don't tie someone up and throw him in a ditch, even if he committed a violent crime. But in a philosophy class, this probably wouldn't even be mentioned by the philosophy instructor, or it would just be glossed over or dismissed. Socrates doesn't seem to have a problem with the father's actions, or at least the question of the father's guilt doesn't interest him. Just like a Hollywood film where everyone roots for the pre-determined hero, the philosopher today unthinkingly roots for Socrates, misses some of his flaws, and makes him bigger than life, larger than a mere mortal.

Where the philosopher has a point is in the fact that Euthyphro's justification for going against his father is rather weak. He does say that a murderer should be punished, but he seems more interested in justifying his action by stating that the gods often challenge or "go against" their fathers. But that's understandable. Religious people have trouble explaining the world outside of their supernatural beliefs. "What would Jesus do?" sounds like something Euthyphro would say. And in Euthyphro's assertion that Greek gods challenged their fathers, he is on solid ground. In fact, throughout Greek cosmology, there's a tradition of it, and, of course, with the Ancient Greeks it's often spicy: Cronos cutting off the genitals of Uranus and throwing them into a pond to give birth to Aphrodite, or Zeus disguised as a potion-maker releasing his siblings from his father's belly and starting a ten-year war until the Olympians ultimately take down the Titans and settle Greek cosmology. Today a Christian might admit that God is the father of Satan, and Satan challenged God according to Christian doctrine. And Adam and Eve didn't listen to God so well either. But in any case, Socrates's point is that while these may be interesting stories, they are not philosophically sound reasons to do or not do something.

But we don't have to just give examples from the mythic and supernatural realms. Today we are seeing that suing one's relatives and even one's parents can be done. The idea of suing one's parents is not unheard of and, I suspect, will become more commonplace. From asking for college tuition to demanding punishment for abuse, we hear about it on the news regularly. It seems that we will see more and more children challenging their parents. Of course, there are good and bad aspects of this. Parents need to be held accountable, yet they also need to be able to exert rational authority over their children in order for their children to grow, mature, and develop into responsible adults.

4

One under-discussed issue concerning the idea of holding parents responsible is the debate that occurred about the NFL star running back Adrian Peterson. Peterson is an extraordinary football player. He was accused and found guilty of abusing one of his children. It's interesting because, while the general consensus is that Peterson crossed a line in punishing his child (he stripped the leaves off a stick and stuffed them in the four-year-old's mouth, then hit him in problematic places with that stick, among other things), the general consensus still is that it's perfectly fine to spank children. But is it really? In the case of Peterson, his son didn't even live with him or see him on a daily basis. Getting beaten by someone who is your father, but who doesn't take on the day-to-day responsibilities of a father, seems especially sad and cruel. Clearly being abused in this way would be somewhat terrifying for a child.

If we step back for a second we can see that it's rather crazy to think that this is even debatable. Spanking, hitting, striking with a belt, giving a whipping, using a switch, etc., on a child is clearly barbaric. It is intrinsically cruel. It doesn't work as effective punishment, and most likely increases anti-social behavior, aggression, mental health problems, and cognitive struggles.[1] Still, Americans love to spank and hit their children. Most parents still use some sort of violence to discipline their children, and most people believe, "done properly," it is legitimate. Many, and actually most child beaters, claim to be religious. Yet if we think about it for just a moment, it is clearly not an ideal thing to do. In fact, it's a pretty rotten thing to do in almost all circumstances. To hit, spank, whack, beat, use a switch, hand or anything else on a small and vulnerable person is cruel. Spanking is what people do when they are not smart enough, or nice enough, or creative enough, to discipline in an ethical or rational way. Spanking is at best dumb and cruel, and at worst evil and sadistic. It is an immature action that runs the gamut of childish lashing out to sadistic torture. Yet, sadly, my claim that spanking is barbaric will be counterintuitive to most people today. By comparison, Liberals sometimes say that abortion should be legal, but rare. Conservatives say it should be illegal. Well, at best, spanking should be legal but rare, and actually it should probably be illegal. It is clearly immoral.

Perhaps conservatives should first show more care for sentient beings than non-sentient ones if they want to claim some sort of moral authority on the abortion issue. Let's start by all agreeing not to spank children and then, when we get that straight, we can start to have a conversation about non-sentient beings, about fetuses.

5

Just as most people today will roll their eyes when they hear someone claim that spanking a child is wrong, most Greeks rolled their eyes when someone said a citizen should be held accountable for the death of a slave. I'm sure many plantation owners rolled their eyes, too, when someone suggested that slavery was wrong, or that their Christian beliefs contradicted the idea that it's OK to own human beings. Perhaps slave owners should be spanked. In any case, like Southern plantation owners, most people in Ancient Greece didn't take the rights of the Other seriously. Ironically, the wisdom that Euthyphro's father was guilty of something was put in the mouth of an idiot. Should his father have been accused of murder? Probably not. But he was definitely guilty of something. And in the Ancient Greek legal system, murdering a slave would only have been punished with a minor penalty anyway, such as paying a fine. It's not as if Euthyphro's father would have really been in trouble, even if his son had won the case against him. Euthyphro suing his father was probably more of a power struggle. But again

---

1 See "Spanking and Child Outcomes: Old Controversies and New Meta-Analyses," Gershoff and Grogan-Kaylor, in Journal of Family Psychology, April 7, 2016.

Plato's brilliance comes through in the story because even the character Euthyphro, in his own way, is well-rounded; he holds a certain interest despite his weakness in formulating and analyzing philosophical arguments. Among the many lessons embedded in the character of Euthyphro is that one can get something correct, yet for the wrong reasons; and we can miss some obvious wisdom when it comes out of the mouth of an idiot (there's probably a lesson concerning Donald Trump here). Plato was the master of esoteric teachings, sometimes so esoteric he himself didn't see it.

6

My idiot high school basketball coach used to say, "every once in a while a blind squirrel finds an acorn." Maybe Euthyphro just got lucky in making us think more deeply. But because basketball is a great player-driven game, bad coaches can collect acorns; they can still win some games and pass on some knowledge — and because Plato is a great philosopher, we can learn from a character such as Euthyphro. A simple and self-deluded character, a Euthyphro, can provoke new thoughts in us. And we can separate what we learn without having to like or accept the rest of what Euthyphro says.

In this spirit let's turn back to the master coach, the Phil Jackson Zen Master of the ancient world, Socrates, and engage with his dialectical method. Let's turn back to philosophy proper and focus on what matters for the philosopher. What matters for the philosopher are the reasons for belief, more than the specific belief itself. The structure of argument is more important than the conclusion, when "doing" philosophy. There are important reasons for this. Anyone can get lucky in drawing a conclusion, but we want to be sure our conclusions come from solid premises; we want our premises to lead to our conclusions. We want our arguments to hold together, we want our premises to be true, and we want them to logically lead to the conclusion. And that's the big problem with Euthyphro. Overall, his arguments and his reasoning are really not sound, and he has no other rational or moral insights in the dialogue, including failing to question the morality of slavery. The fact that he may have been on to something in trying to hold his father responsible proves to be extremely limiting; it's a rather small acorn.

What was really driving Euthyphro was fear of the gods. He thought that the gods would punish him if he didn't sue his father. This is silly and yet interesting. Still today we have human beings making decisions that affect real human lives, based on beliefs about supernatural beings. This is the real philosophically interesting insight in the *Euthyphro*. Plato gets us reflecting on why and how we justify our actions. Socrates is thinking about the bigger picture, and he wants us to think about whether or not it's wise to justify ourselves by appealing to the gods. Should we really do something based on the reason that we are afraid of the gods or we want to please the gods? The dialogue form, as well as the specific content, gives Plato an opportunity to take us on a dialectical journey into this question. In a version of determinate negation, Socrates questions supernatural explanations and challenges explanations based on authority alone. The questioning and challenging come through Socrates, as if from reason itself. Socrates himself is a determinate negation. He is the determinate counterexample, in both content and form, to the irrationality in Ancient Greece.

Like so many people in positions of power today, Euthyphro fancies himself wise because he is an authority figure; he sees himself as a priest-like sage who has an in with the gods. Listening to Euthyphro, one gets the image of the unctuous Mike Huckabee. Euthyphro is more than willing to tell Socrates all that he is privy to, but Socrates isn't interested in his stories. Euthyphro enjoys gossip, religious gossip. Often the loudest, most confident voices in society are the most vacuous and Socrates intuitively senses the emptiness in Euthyphro. Still, Euthyphro's willingness to spread his "knowledge" gives Socrates the opportunity for a teaching moment, a Socratic, proto-Hegelian, dialectical, teaching moment. But this teaching moment would probably occur over a glass of wine rather than a beer.

7

Hegel's famous dialectic in the *Science of Logic* begins with the most abstract concept, that of "being." Plato's dialogue *Euthyphro*, in like fashion, starts with the most abstract notion of piety. Socrates and Euthyphro both agree, at the beginning of the inquiry, that there is a form of piety such that all instances of piety will fit into it. The form piety captures all pious acts, as being captures all that is. As being is existence, it captures all particular beings, and as the form of piety is piety, it captures all particular instances of piety. Both are abstractions hiding something as they feign totality; both deny an outside as they promote identity between individual instance and abstract definition.

Yet the outside cannot be denied. "Being" invokes the idea of nothing. To grasp "being" one must grasp the concept nothing. "Piety," understood as an essential definition, invokes impiety. To grasp "piety" one must grasp impiety. Plato gives this concrete life in Euthyphro's prosecution of his father; it is both pious and impious. In both the cases of Hegel and Plato, conceptualization is not the main or driving point. Concepts only become concepts through a dialectical process, a dialectical process that precedes conceptualization. From the start, for anything to be intelligible at all, it must be differentiated from other things. Ideas and objects need contrast to come into being as the ideas or objects we know them as. This contrast might be seeing one object as distinct from others or it might be seeing an object as more than that object; in other words, seeing that object as transcendent in some sense. Horkheimer and Adorno, in *Dialectic of Enlightenment*, use the example of the word "tree" to show how language makes a tree more than a tree. Subjects, using language, have the ability to "make" a tree something spiritual, or a metaphor, or into a weapon, or into shelter, or part of a forest, or mere wood, or a species, and even into a story. Every tree has a story. Through language objects become more than objects, as we link them to other things, including, but not necessarily, conceptualizing them. Language may even be the condition of possibility to see a tree as a tree, to differentiate it as an independent entity in the forest. Language helps us see the tree as less than the forest and more than the branches. Even our identities are formed dialectically. Different individuals in a classroom are linked by sharing in the concept "student." One becomes a student as one stops being merely an individual. Yet that student is still an individual. But now her individuality also includes her student-ness. Being a student adds to her individuality. The concept of individuality now contains student-ness, as being a student contains the idea of an individual. Yet neither can be reduced to the other. The concept student replaces the person as mere individual, so in this sense one only becomes a student as one is un-becoming an individual, and yet, because this person is an individual, this person can also be a student.

Piety, then, is not just what it is; it is also what it is not. Piety is a concept and hence is abstract; and there are instances of piety, and hence it is concrete. Euthyphro, being concerned with his own self, defines piety as something concrete; he equates it with his own action. He says piety is: "to do what I am doing now."[1] He thinks he's prosecuting a wrongdoer. He justifies his actions by claiming that the gods challenge and even go against their fathers, so he can too. While Socrates doubts this claim about the gods, he does show that, even if Euthyphro is correct, at best Euthyphro is only giving an example of piety and not a universal definition of piety. Yet Euthyphro's definition moves the dialectic. As being invokes the idea of nothing, a search for a universal definition of piety invokes a particular, concrete instance, and perhaps a dubious instance of piety. In this way there is something correct in Euthyphro's first definition of piety despite the fact that his initial try, his example about himself trying to justify himself, is the farthest possible distance from an abstract, essential definition.

---

1 Plato, *The Trial and Death of Socrates*, p. 6.

8

Although Euthyphro's definition of piety as "doing what I'm doing" does not capture all individual instances of piety (in fact, it's the exact opposite of that), it still moves the dialectic forward so that even Euthyphro himself can see that he must do better. His better is to claim that piety is "what is dear to the gods."[1] If Hegel's dialectic of being and nothing gives way to becoming, then piety becomes a type of becoming through the gods. Piety comes into being with the gods; it is doing what is dear to the gods. Piety is what is dear to the gods and these fickle, unpredictable gods are the link to a religious devotion whose rules seem to change with the wind. What is pious today may not be pious tomorrow, for no one knows the whims of the gods. To be pious, should I pray, sacrifice, rely on grace, good works, give indulgences, pursue success, claim victory, retreat from the world, become a poet, priest, or pilot? Should I have rags or riches, wives or a wife, children or remain chaste? There is something distressingly and historically accurate about pulling piety into the vicissitudes of supernatural history. Piety has often been defined as "what is dear to the gods" and what is dear to the gods flows like the Nile River ... and sometimes dries up. As a rationalist, Socrates points out that the gods seem to disagree all the time, so which god to choose? It's similar to trying to pick which parts of the Bible to emphasize today, wondering if the Old Testament need be taken literally, and so on. If you just choose the god (or the parts of the scriptures) suited to your interests it's hard to claim you are doing the ethical thing. And if the gods disagree among themselves, then the definition of piety, "doing what's dear to the gods," seems to be a logical contradiction. If some gods find it endearing and others don't, then the same act can be good and bad at the same time. This is no good.

9

Socrates and Euthyphro modify the definition by adding one word. They agree, for the moment, that perhaps "the pious is what all the gods love."[2] By adding the word "all" they resolve the logical contradiction. Now it seems something is good or pious when all the gods agree it is, and something is bad or impious when they all say it's impious. And in terms of the things the gods cannot agree on, well then, who knows. But this definition is ambiguous in that the question arises, "Is the pious being loved by the gods because it is pious, or is it pious because it is being loved by the gods?" It becomes a

---

1 Ibid., p. 7.
2 All of my quotations in this section from Plato are from *The Trial and Death of Socrates*, p. 11.

kind of "chicken or egg" problem. Is something pious only because the gods decide it is, or is piety somehow outside the gods and perhaps above them? Do the gods themselves aim to live up to piety? Evolution implies that the egg came first, and Socrates and Euthyphro agree that virtues are prior to, or at least anterior to the gods — piety is higher than the gods. This is not to say that gods are chickens, but like chickens, they came out of something else — they hatched from a human egghead. The point though is that Socrates and Euthyphro agree that piety, as concept, is outside the gods, and so saying the gods find piety dear is simply to give an attribute or characteristic of piety. It's no better than saying basketball is that sport Tom likes; he finds it dear. At this point in the discussion a wise interlocutor would not try to define piety in terms of the gods anymore; but Euthyphro is not much wiser than a chicken.

In the Middle Ages even the great minds basically found it impossible to conceive of philosophy without religion. They regressed back to the supernatural. The medieval mind, unlike the Ancient Greek mind, could only conceive of God as both chicken and egg. History and conceptual thinking is not always linear and it is not always forward moving. We can lose the gains we make in life and in philosophy. The Classical Greek Age took some freedom away from women compared to the Bronze Age, and philosophy in the Middle Ages took some philosophical freedom away from philosophy. Philosophers in the Middle Ages limited themselves by insisting that God was the absolute foundation; God was everything. Today analytic philosophers move philosophy backwards with their insistence on ahistorical, conceptual analysis and otherworldly puzzles. Taking dialectics out of philosophy is analogous to taking art out of life. We know that philosophy is an historical activity and is more art than science, so why deny the richness of philosophy? Why be so afraid to leave the cave, or the coop? Perhaps, unlike Socrates, most philosophers are more chicken than egghead.

10

Socrates refuses to handicap philosophy, and as a dialectical thinker he continues the conversation despite Euthyphro's inability to think without appealing to the supernatural. Socrates moves the dialogue along by asking if piety might not be connected to justice. To further delink the concept from religion, Socrates paradoxically quotes the wisdom of Zeus, who says that "where there is fear there is also shame."[1] Then he quickly adds, "I disagree with the poet." Socrates, the master ironist, is reminding us we can disagree with the gods. The gods do not live in the house of truth. According to Socrates, while it is true that fear and shame are related, they cannot be reduced to

1 Ibid., p. 14.

the same thing. How are they related? Which is the bigger concept? Fear is bigger. One can be afraid without feeling shame. One can just be afraid. But we cannot feel shame unless we are also afraid. Shame is a part of fear, but not the whole part. In the funny Seinfeld episode where Jerry's supermodel girlfriend thinks she catches Jerry picking his nose, he feels shame because he is afraid she will break up with him for it. He feels shame despite the fact he was only scratching his nose. Still, he would feel no shame if he had picked his nose without anyone seeing. The show "Fraser" also played on the gaze of the Other and the relationship between fear and shame. Fraser was bothered by the gaze of his father's dog on him. The dog made him feel shame because he, for some reason, feared the dog at some level. He thought the dog was judging him. Euthyphro should feel shame for suing his father but he doesn't. Because he only fears the non-existent gods, who are believed by Euthyphro and others to challenge each other regardless of the ethics, he doesn't fear his father or the opinions of the Greeks. Without a modicum of fear or respect for other people, he is shameless. We see that fear can be a good thing. Not just in the obvious sense that we should fear things that can harm us. Fear, in many instances, can be rational. And of course some fears are irrational. Further, we should fear certain things, things like the possibility that our actions are harming others, or the possibility that we are doing something wrong. When we don't care about other people, and when we don't care about whether we are doing something correctly (meaning we could be harming others), we lose the ability to feel shame when we do harm others. This is dangerous and it shows a lack of human virtue.

If one feels shame toward a god, that's just weird. It's not real; it's an indirect or unreflective way of being narcissistic. The metaphysical urge distorts shame and fear so that we don't feel them or experience them when it's humanly kind to do so. Thus many who follow a god are afraid of what this god might do to them, or what this god might think about them; and this can trump how they treat other people. We have all experienced the sad situation when someone goes over everyone else's head because that person is supposedly following God. It's ugly. And they feel no shame from it because they have lost the humanistic ability to view life in relation to concrete others and to understand what really matters. It is an immature rationalization that allows them to be selfish but to think of themselves as virtuous. Rather than engaging others who are affected by their choice, they "pray on it." They view their life through their fantasy of what God or "their truth" demands of them, which allows them to do what they really wish to do deep down, regardless of its virtue, and at the same time it allows them to escape taking responsibility for it, by passing the buck to their god.

From a purely logical perspective Socrates makes clear the relation between part and whole at this juncture of the argument. He gives the example of numbers and points out the fact that every odd number is also a number, but not every number is an odd number. Where there is an odd number there is a number, but where there is a number there may not be an odd number. "Number" is the larger concept. This helps Euthyphro understand the puzzle concerning the relationship between piety and justice. Getting back to piety, then, Socrates and Euthyphro conclude that justice is the bigger concept and that piety is a part of justice. Justice deals with many things. One can be just or unjust toward oneself, towards others, nature, animals, and other aspects of the world, and even the possible or future world. But piety deals with a specific sort of justice. Piety, the word, by definition, is related to the supernatural; it means to be or act in a religious manner. One could plausibly argue that it seems obvious that piety is justice toward the gods or doing what the gods want one to do. But at this point in the dialectic, piety has already been delinked from the gods, as definition three showed that piety is anterior to the gods.

11

By having Euthyphro as Socrates's interlocutor, Plato is able to write esoterically. Euthyphro refuses to delink piety from the supernatural, as many of his readers would also refuse to do; so Plato can keep them reading while, at the same time, esoterically saying more about piety than a supernatural discussion would allow for. He can say more by dropping hints, through the voice of Socrates, through irony and the feigning of ignorance. These Socratic techniques are part of a Socratic dialogic style. Socrates can talk about piety to those who stay attached to the traditional definition of the concept and, at the same time, he can say more. Still, what exactly does the traditional definition mean? Euthyphro suggests that gods and humans have a relationship, a type of "trading skill,"[1] whereas each side is just toward the other. How can we be just toward the gods? Euthyphro says our justice towards the gods comes in doing the proper prayers and sacrifices. This makes sense from a traditional religious standpoint. We are just toward the gods when we honor them in the way they want to be honored. For the Ancient Greeks that meant prayer and sacrifice. For some today it means ringing strangers' doorbells and spreading the good news. For others it's charity work (or un-charity work, as in denying marriage licenses to citizens). Some today pray, or meditate, or fast, or go to church on Sundays, and others shoot doctors or behead infidels.

---

1 Ibid., p. 18.

In any case, knowing how to give gods their justice is a tricky business. Gods never seem to directly tell us what they want, and there seems to be no consensus about it, no agreement on what it means to be holy. We cannot even agree when and where the gods communicate with us. Are the voices in one's head from God; is the Bible the word of God; does God speak through nature? We can go on and on, but it is fascinating to see the stories people tell themselves to justify their preferred manner of knowing what God wants, who God is, and how God communicates. Some people base their belief in God on their own study, or their upbringing, and some even have doctorates in theology. But isn't getting a Ph.D. in theology kind of like becoming a Grand Dragon of the KKK? Becoming a leader and expert on white supremacy by being educated by those who preach white supremacy, and then being awarded the highest title by the Klan, is clearly in conflict with truth. Just as no one in the KKK takes the idea of racial equality seriously, those in Theology and Religious Studies programs only play pretend doubt. Schopenhauer's line about needing a cure more than a refutation just leaps into the mind.

The point is that, in the end, even if gods existed we could do nothing for them. The gods don't need our prayers, our sacrifices, our charity, or our destructive behavior in their name. We can make up any trade we want to and claim it's for the gods. We hear some holy people say God wants them to be rich, and even to own private jets. It's clear many religious leaders have understood this sort of "guidance" from the beginning and have used it to manipulate the masses. But the foolish followers continue to buy this line of talk, so the leaders keep selling it. Euthyphro is forced to admit that, at best, the gods find our worship of them "pleasing." We have little to trade with the gods. The gods might say —Isn't that cute, the little humans are bargaining with us again.

Still, even if we cannot really do anything for the gods, what can gods do for us? How can the gods be just toward us? According to Euthyphro, the gods are just toward us when they protect our family and our state. We need and want the gods to preserve our life and the lives of those we love and care about. This makes sense. Life is difficult. Death stinks. If by giving a little sacrifice or saying a quick prayer I can be safe and those I care about can be safe, then that's a good deal. Some have even pushed it so far that they have convinced themselves that a quick line, perhaps "Jesus I accept you into my heart as my lord and savior," will land them a ticket to heavenly immortality and a golden house in heaven. It's comparable to getting a golden ticket to Willy Wonka Wonderland. Buy a candy bar, hope for some luck, and you are through the gates. Careful what you wish for, though. God's Chocolate Factory may not be what you imagine. You might just end up with diabetes.

Still, many so-called adults really believe the line, "She's in a better place now." At most, after departing from the holy, one might think, she's in a smarter place now. Of course it's understood that people are trying to cope with loss when they say such things. But we must prefer the truth. When a good person dies, we are all in a worse place. The person is gone forever. She is worse off and everyone who cares about her is worse off.

12

It bears repeating — death stinks. Humans know this and will do about anything to avoid it; if you doubt this check out the Google immortality project. As a response to an existential fear, the dream of an afterlife is understandable. It may not be very plausible, but if it's true, that's awesome; and if not, at least it eases the mind. In the dialogue this takes the form of considering how gods can protect one's family and state, one's society. Euthyphro is convinced the gods can help protect people. Today this is captured in the phrase "God Bless America." We see in this entreaty that even today we fear that we need help from the outside, from higher up, to be safe. This reminds us of the true cause of belief in the supernatural. The parts of life that seem too much for us, that seem out of our control or beyond our understanding, give rise to supernatural beliefs. We try to control the unknown by giving it an agent's attributes. This way we can attempt to communicate with it and save ourselves. We are willing to worship it, if it will help us. Many people prefer to believe that our ideas about God stemmed from love and gratitude, but it's really about protection and fear when we say "God Bless America." It's a tribal response to fear. Even the modern world is tribal.

In this way we can say we have a split attitude toward modernity. On the one hand, we love what the modern world has given us. On the other hand, we don't quite trust it, and we feel we are betraying something in our past when we accept modernity. We counter the spleen by criticizing the government as a sport. Turn on talk radio and you can hear the game. It's play. In the modern world we love to complain about the government; we enjoy pretending we could survive without our modern institutions. But it's only because modern societies are so amazing that we can do so with such abandon. From our schools to our cultural institutions to our laws and justice system, we are doing pretty well in relation to the totality of the human comedy. And the opportunities for becoming the person one wants to become are there for more people than ever. We are a long, long way from being where we can and should be, but nonetheless modernity rocks in light of human history. Still, we have not come to terms with our past and the feeling of spleen sustains, whether those ditto-heads listening to the radio acknowledge it or not.

Socrates is reminding Euthyphro, and us, that it is really important not just to use our society and not just to complain about it. Don't just destroy tradition, but also don't follow it blindly. And he is suggesting that it is rather naïve to simply pray that things will get better. We need to be the agents who protect our family and state. The job is ours, not the gods'. If you want to make a sacrifice, then sacrifice for your family or country, not for the gods. Supernatural beings don't need you. While Socrates demystifies the notion that to be pious is to sacrifice to supernatural beings, he does not directly give a positive definition of piety. Yet, in his esoteric way, he does hint that piety is sacrificing for one's family and state. Euthyphro, who continues to want to sue his father, clearly misses this suggestion. At one level the dialogue is a failure, but for those looking a little beneath the surface we see that Socrates is articulating an important truth. Caring for your family and state is part of living a just life. We should call that piety, for metaphorically, it is a religious or holy sacrifice. You give some of your life to your family and society, you sacrifice for them. While what is usually taken as piety, praying and sacrificing to supernatural beings, and doing things in the name of gods, is a shameful game of pretend.

13

We are not surprised that Euthyphro doesn't get it. He runs away from the conversation. People don't like to hear what they don't want to hear. Ideas that challenge one's ideology, or when a useful approach to problem solving entails more work than simply praying, sacrificing, or chanting, these challenges often get rationalized away. Euthyphro prefers to give monologues and not be questioned. It's not always easy to justify oneself in dialogue with others, and it's not always fun to compromise. Euthyphro wants to quit the dialogue since it didn't go his way on the first attempt. Not Socrates. He wants to keep the conversation going. Try again. Maybe fail again. But as Samuel Beckett said — fail better. Socrates is willing to risk failure for the chance to get things right and to help Euthyphro see truth. That's the Socratic spirit, and it spooks Euthyphro more than any ghost could hope to do, so he runs away from the conversation.

As a work of art, though, *Euthyphro* is brilliant; a negative ending in the spirit of Adorno's negative dialectics, a proto-negative dialectics so to speak. By being pulled up short, by not smoothing over the contradictions, by speaking on different levels and to different audiences, this text opens the philosophical mind. It ends in failure, since no definitive definition is produced, and yet we sense what a beautifully pious life could be. Socrates lived that life. Socrates sacrificed for the youth, for his city. The text shows us that something is itself and is not itself. And yet, the reader today knows that Socrates had his flaws too. He was not a great husband. His life was pious and not pious. Still, to get a glimpse of Socrates's idea of a non-religious piety it helps to see Euthyphro's confident belief that a pious life consists in giving prayers and sacrifices to the gods, to see Euthyphro's naïve assertion that life in service of supernatural beings is worthwhile. All the while Euthyphro made those around him worse, Socrates made the youth better; and he made them better through concrete, relevant dialogue, not abstract, theoretical monologue. Socrates, then, as determinate negation, not only deconstructs Euthyphro but also deconstructs formal Platonic philosophy.

14

If the vision of Socrates that comes through in the *Euthyphro* is one of a man in search of a universal definition, then we can contrast it with the *Apology*. The *Apology* is anything but an apology and anything but a search for a universal definition.

The Greek "apologia" is the meaning here; Plato is offering an account and a defense, not an apology. It's a double — double — double. Neither Socrates nor Plato will apologize, and we will get two accounts, one where Socrates offers up his own autobiography, the other, an account of the trial. Further, we get a two-fold defense; one of Socrates the man, one of philosophy as vocation. This is all mediated through the drama of a trial. First we see Socrates approaching the problem of his trial in an unusual way. Rather than employing rhetoric in the standard ways, Socrates claims to just speak the truth, to seek the truth rather than attempt to win his case. Seeking truth means engaging others in dialogue, even those trying to destroy him, even the man prosecuting him. Socrates wants his community to judge him, for he understands we are the world's only judges. He says "concentrate your attention on whether what I say is just or not."[1]

Socrates employs his version of philosophical genealogy by going back 40 years to explain his reputation. He knows that to understand who he is, what he's about, and what constitutes philosophy, we need an historical narrative. He calls those who didn't respect him, who lied about him, his "first accusers." They lie by misrepresenting who he is. Rather than accepting that he is a philosopher, they call him "a wise man, a student of all things in the sky and below the earth, who makes the worse argument the stronger." In other words they accuse him of being a sophist, a scientist, or a rhetorician.

---

1 All of my quotations in this section from Plato are from *The Trial and Death of Socrates*, pp. 21–26.

They want to reduce him to a stereotypical atheist. His accusers "believe that those who study these things do not even believe in the gods." Notice that he never gets accused of being a poet or a holy man. In Ancient Greece, philosophy and religion were at odds; Plato claims, in *The Republic*, that there was an ancient quarrel between philosophy and poetry. We should take his claim of an ancient quarrel with a grain of salt if we are literally thinking about historical time, for philosophy was not ancient yet — but it is spot on when we think conceptually. Philosophy and religion are conceptually, from the beginning, opposed. And more importantly, only one is dialectically inclined. Religion believes in beginnings, begins with a beginning — IN THE BEGINNING. Dialectical philosophy "begins" (ironically, as the ancient epics told by poets) — in *medias res*.

Socrates says that what gave him his reputation is "a certain kind of wisdom." It is what he calls "human wisdom," unlike the Sophists who, he sarcastically says, "are wise with a wisdom more than human." Socrates's quest to understand the meaning of his human wisdom began around the time he was 30, and it was motivated by Chaerephon asking the god at Delphi if anyone was wiser than Socrates. The god said no, and Socrates set out to prove the god wrong. We see the irony in Socrates taking the gods seriously enough to consider the truth of their wisdom but not so seriously as to accept the god's claim. In any case, it motivates Socrates's quest. He searches for someone wiser than himself — to refute the god — and after witnessing the lack of wisdom in the person with the reputation for being wisest, Socrates waded through the politicians, the poets, and the craftsmen searching for someone wiser than himself, but without success. The poets did speak well about the important things, but they could not articulate the meaning. They seemed to be driven by "inborn talent and by inspiration." The craftsmen did have specific knowledge of their crafts, and in that surpassed Socrates, but like the politicians, who were good orators, they made the mistake of thinking that their craft or the knowledge of their vocation gave them insight into deeper, more human wisdom. Being a good politician or a skilled worker is not the wisdom Socrates was trying to discover. If none of these groups have philosophical wisdom, then it turns out that no one is really wise. This allows Socrates to interpret the god's claim that he is wiser than everyone else as meaning that human wisdom is worthless, in one sense. Human wisdom is worthless to gods, for human wisdom doesn't concern gods. It transcends religion.

When Socrates says it's worthless, what he means is similar to someone responding with "I'm nothing" when asked what religion he or she is. Socrates is wisest because he knows nothing and knows he knows nothing. In other words, he is aware of the dialectical complexity of knowledge. Those around him unreflectively are confident in their beliefs; they think they know things, and in their hubris they miss how complicated things are. Today, American students globally rank rather low in math and science knowledge, and yet they are unmatched in confidence and self-esteem when it comes to what they think they know. The average Athenian would fit in well here. Against this hubris, Socrates's reflective act — knowing nothing, and knowing that he knows nothing — is not worthless and is not ignorance. Knowing that he knows nothing is knowledge, and it is both intrinsically worthwhile and instrumentally relevant. It is intrinsically worthwhile as Socrates is happy, content, and living in the moment. He is living his final ends. He is grounded. He understands himself and the human condition, and how fallible and finite we are. This wisdom allows Socrates to be internally harmonious. His theory matches the practice of being human; his beliefs are concretely reflected in his actions. And instrumentally it has kept him safe and allowed him to thrive in Athens his whole life. Remember, he became conscious of his "human wisdom" at age thirty and has lived the last forty years his way. He did not waste his life. His beliefs and his actions fit into a coherent whole. Socrates is not a torn soul. He is not working in a job exploiting others; he is not alienated from himself, others, or his world. He is not driving a Hummer H3 with NOTW (Not of this World) plastered on the back window. He is not absurd.

Initially it seems that being the wisest of the unwise is nothing to write home about. But it turns out to be something very worthwhile. This sort of wisdom, non-wisdom, still is dangerous without power. Some around Socrates are jealous, even of his negative virtue. Try saying "I'm nothing" next time somebody asks you if you are a Christian, and you will understand. Your modesty will probably be interpreted as an attack. Those who fake it, those who have convinced others they are wise, are exposed during a Socratic quest. They have disdain for those who dare to not play their games. As Socrates said these kinds of "people are ambitious, violent, and numerous" and are willing to crush anyone who exposes them. This made Socrates's philosophical quest a dangerous one. Philosophy as a critical and reflective action is not a simple debate about belief; it is revolutionary activity that can get one killed.

15

It's not until after this long introduction on his life and history that Socrates gets to the official or formal charges against him. He breaks them down into three distinct statements: corrupting the youth, not believing in the gods of his city, and having his own divinities. He starts with the corruption charge and uses it to give an instance of the practice of philosophy. By asking Meletus questions, he initiates the dialectic. Since Meletus claims to know who corrupts the youth, he asks Meletus who makes the youth better. Meletus initially gives a reified answer as he says the laws. Socrates pushes the dialectic into the human sphere so that Meletus modifies his answer to "everyone but Socrates improves the youth."[1] Clearly we have sarcasm going on, but there is a deeper point. We get definition by negative contrast that in turn refutes itself by being false. Meletus contrasts everyone in the city to Socrates and then is forced into the conclusion that, since Meletus claims the youth have been corrupted, either Socrates is more powerful (he's almost supernatural) than everyone else in the city combined, or the whole city is so pitifully weak that it cannot stop a seventy-year-old man from corrupting its youth. This is absurd. Yet Plato is also able to show the power of philosophy. When one has the right philosophy, when theory and practice are harmoniously united, then it does become the most powerful thing. Truth is the most powerful thing. Meletus's absurd claim, that everyone but Socrates improves the youth, exposes Meletus's false representation of the dialectic. Socrates exposes Meletus's lack of interest in truth, his dependence on authority, and his disregard for the youth. By pushing Meletus into an absurd statement, "everyone but Socrates makes the youth better," Socrates shows that Meletus is not concerned with the youth or the good of the city. Meletus is using the legal system to promote his own private, conservative interests. Apparently some things never change.

Socrates further explores the dialectic between the few and the many through an analogy of caring for horses. In the case of horses, it is the horse breeder who makes horses better whereas the majority without knowledge "corrupts horses." This example would be familiar to his audience and noncontroversial. Trust the horse breeder and trainer rather than the rabble when it comes to horses. By analogy, then, Socrates is suggesting that one should not trust the majority's opinion when it comes to what or who corrupts the youth, nor should one trust that the masses are actually protecting the youth. In this way the dialectic advances from scapegoating Socrates to the obligations of everyone in the city. What started as an attack on an individual for corrupting the youth has turned into a referendum on everyone in the city. If the youth are corrupted, clearly it is not simply Socrates's fault.

---

1 All of my quotations in this section from Plato are from *The Trial and Death of Socrates*, pp. 27–29.

Meletus is trying to propagate beliefs that are not consistent with reality or logic. Socrates exposes Meletus's faulty logic by starting with a series of seemingly innocuous and seemingly irrelevant questions. Using an indirect method he asks rhetorical questions, beginning with "is it better for a man to live among good or wicked fellow citizens?" and Meletus is forced to answer that we all prefer good neighbors. Then Socrates asks, "Is there any man who wants to be harmed?" Meletus concedes that no one intentionally harms himself. Finally Socrates asks for clarification insofar as his motives. He asks whether he corrupts the youth "intentionally or unintentionally?" Meletus says that Socrates is intentionally harming the youth. The end result of these rapid-fire questions is that Meletus is pretty much forced to make and accept three statements: 1. We all prefer good neighbors. 2. No one intentionally harms himself. 3. Socrates is intentionally corrupting the youth.

But logically one cannot hold all three statements together. If we all want good neighbors, and if Socrates doesn't want harm to come to him, then he would not deliberately corrupt the youth. Or, if we all want good neighbors, and yet Socrates corrupted the youth, then Socrates must want to harm himself. Or if Socrates does not want to harm himself, and he wants to corrupt the youth, then we don't all want good neighbors. Since all three statements cannot be true together, Socrates argues that he must not be corrupting the youth, or if he is corrupting them then it must be unintentional. If it's the former, he should be found innocent, and if the latter he should be educated as to how he's corrupting them rather than being prosecuted and punished.

16

Today many people believe that atheists are immoral. Then they might meet someone they consider a good person only to find out later that this person is an atheist. Now they are in a situation comparable to that above. They are holding on to three beliefs: 1. All atheists are immoral. 2. Person *x* is moral. 3. Person *x* is an atheist. Holding on to all three of these statements is contradictory. If it's true that all atheists are immoral, and that person *x* is an atheist, then person *x* is actually immoral. Or person *x* is an atheist, and person *x* is moral, then not all atheists are immoral. Or perhaps all atheists are immoral, and person *x* is moral, then that person is really not an atheist. Test this theory and you will be surprised by how many people hold all three statements to be true, or prefer to deny statement two or three rather than give up statement one. It is hardest to get religious people to drop the first claim. Ironically, most recent studies show that non-religious people, including non-religious children, are more ethically inclined than religious people.[1]

17

In any case, Socrates's method is smart and clever, and still useful today, but his audience was filled with Euthyphro types so he was fighting an uphill battle. But Socrates really was trying to help the youth; he spent the bulk of his life caring for the youth; he took the corruption charge seriously. The other two charges were of less interest to him.

Still, Socrates quickly refutes the last two charges in a similar manner, highlighting the strength of reason and the usefulness of philosophy. First he asks for clarification concerning the first charge. When Meletus claims Socrates doesn't believe in the gods of the state, does this mean Socrates is an atheist, or does it mean Socrates believes in other gods? Meletus says it's the former; he claims Socrates is an atheist. Now to be an atheist at Socrates's time didn't necessarily mean not believing in gods at all. It might have meant that Socrates didn't worship or follow any specific gods. Socrates may just think the gods are irrelevant or not concerned with human things. The idea that the gods were distant and unconcerned with humans, in the way that Lucretius later articulated it, would not be foreign to Socrates, and these types would also be labeled as atheists. In any case, Socrates denies being an atheist, and further, he tries to show that Meletus contradicts himself since the third charges is that Socrates has his own divinities. In other words, Socrates is less concerned with the charge and more interested in showing Meletus's lack of reasoning skills. Socrates asks how is it possible for one to be an atheist if one has other divinities. If Socrates worships or consults spiritual things, then he cannot be an atheist in either the strong or the weak sense. He must believe in gods and he must think they are relevant and helpful. Socrates makes it clear that divinities are a type of spirit, and spiritual activity implies gods. He is Western enough to believe and assert that you can't have spirits or spiritual activity without believing in gods.

Yet the manner in which Socrates is related to the gods takes him beyond religion and away from atheism. Gods are useful metaphors, they offer powerful interpretations for understanding the world, and they can aid in conceptualization. Putting certain attributes into a concrete form — a god — may help one better understand those attributes. But interest in the gods outside of their aid in conceptualization did not seem to interest Socrates. He appealed to the gods but never was interested in them as gods; his focus was on the values linked to them, the ideas that can be enriched through them, rather than in the validity of any specific god's existence. The gods

1 See Sciencemag.org September 11, 2014 and November 5, 2015.

were a bridge, for Socrates, to pull the youth into philosophy. Consider books such as *The Simpsons and Philosophy*. There are tons of this type of book because they use fiction and popular culture to pull people, especially young people, into philosophy. Socrates had at his disposal a rich Greek cosmology, filled with delightful supernatural characters, to help turn the youth toward philosophy. It might have been a technique, since all children would have learned these myths, for Socrates to teach virtue. Starting with the familiar myths, he could move the youth toward unfamiliar philosophical concepts. In fact, Plato, in many dialogues, solidifies his points through both mythos and logos.

In any case, unlike the majority of Ancient Greeks, Socrates seems to have cultivated something of a deep inner self. The typical Greek would not have been very internally motivated or introspective. The Ancient Greeks were an externally focused people and quiet, deep introspection was not their specialty. In fact, as we see in children, in Ancient Greece, when typical Ancient Greeks read something written they would have had to read it out loud to comprehend it. It's not easy to read to oneself, to read in one's mind; children take time to learn this. Perhaps Socrates had cultivated this skill, and with it the skill to be able to look inside himself. Perhaps he had cultivated robust self-reflection, and could watch and think about himself as he acted or spoke. This would make it seem, to those without that skill, that he had a spirit inside him, as if a god were communicating with him. He himself may even have interpreted it that way. Socrates moved beyond belief in spiritual beings and mere atheism as he was able to go deeper into himself and develop himself into a unique and positive creation. And as he went deeper into himself, he was able to connect more deeply to the youth. His abilities and interests transcended the rest of Athens. Like most other Athenians, Socrates did not turn belief into a fetish, but unlike most other Athenians, his actions transcended external success and reward. Socratic actions involve reflection and consciousness and are aimed at internal and intrinsic goods, as much as external and instrumental ones. Socratic reflective acts blend the inner and the outer until that distinction dissolves. The youth could feel the power and virtue of this way of being human, and that's why they followed him. Socrates was comfortable standing under a tree by himself for a full day contemplating philosophy, and just as comfortable engaging in a symposium all night with multiple interlocutors; as he put it, "the life of a philosopher, to examine myself and others."[1] Critical reflection, linked with action, is the Socratic art.

In fact he took his vocation so seriously he called himself a gadfly and the city a slow horse that needed to be kept alert, which needed its consciousness

---

1 Ibid., p. 31.

raised. As gadfly he was an agent in cultivating critical practices. He was so confident in his innocence that he said if anyone had been harmed by him, they should step forward and tell the jury. No one stepped forward, for Socrates did not harm others. Notice that he didn't ask about beliefs, and he didn't ask if he had ever said anything incorrect or untrue; rather he asked if anyone was harmed by him, if anyone's life was ruined.

18

In the second speech Socrates is supposed to articulate a just punishment for himself. He has just been found guilty. The vote was close but nonetheless he is expected to respect the vote, and his peers, and offer up something fair. He rejects exile as an option, for he says he could not do philosophy anywhere else. Again, this shows he is beyond mere belief and ideology. He advocates a philosophy of action. If beliefs are central, one can be anywhere. If God is what matters, one can talk to God anywhere. But Socrates is beyond religious ideology and needs the base of his society to be himself. He cannot leave Athens. He also rejects paying a large sum of money; he refuses to buy his way out of trouble. He doesn't want to act unjustly and he doesn't want to burden his friends. As dialectically astute, he goes beyond rejecting these alternatives and gets provocative. He has the audacity to say, after just being found guilty, that a man like him deserves some good. Akin to the Olympian victor he should be fed in the Prytaneum. The "Olympian victor makes you think yourself happy; I make you be happy."[1] Socrates teaches how to question, reflect, and challenge others and oneself, as he is driven by the insight that for humans "the unexamined life is not worth living." In other words, unlike the athlete or celebrity, the philosopher leads others to their inner and higher humanity. In the case of Socrates, he teaches others how to become themselves through philosophical action. This makes him a type of Olympian, a gold medalist at helping others achieve excellence.

Still, the claim that "the Olympian victor makes you think yourself happy; I make you be happy" would be an outrageous statement to the typical Greek citizen. How dare he compare himself to the city's heroes? But Socrates doesn't say things just to be outrageous. His knowledge is esoteric and by speaking this way he distracts those not worthy of his wisdom. As the rabble around him must have exclaimed, "No, he didn't just say that," the reflective ones realized that he is saying something profound. The Olympic athlete, the celebrity, the successful businessman, and such, do not make us happy; they only give us the feeling of happiness. The Olympic victor's success is not our

1 All of my quotations in this section from Plato are from *The Trial and Death of Socrates*, pp.38–9.

success. We should not live vicariously through others. At best we should take the successful athlete as inspiration to cultivate our own success, our own greatness. But we must be careful not to mistake someone else's success for our own. Human emotions and human communication are tricky things. We cry or get angry during a film that is complete fiction. We think the athlete or celebrity or politician is competing for us, looking at us during the speech, doing it for us. Self-deception is hard to avoid, and Socrates is telling us that not only is someone else's win not our win, but ultimately the other's win will not make us happy. We must create our own lives and create our own happiness. We will waste our lives if we are too fixated on the success of others, or on things that do not exist.

19

In the final speech Socrates says it's easier to avoid death than to avoid wickedness. Socrates is not afraid to tell those who voted him to death that they will not avoid judgment themselves. He says they want him dead because they don't want to examine themselves. Notice his critique is bigger than attacking their abstract beliefs, for he tells them others will follow him, who are stronger and younger, and they will change the city. Perhaps Socrates had a death wish. By dying, he cleared the way for his followers to be more radical. Athens was humiliated for killing an old man who was just asking questions. The city did not have the stomach to go after Socrates's followers even when they were harsher toward the city, even when they pushed philosophy into the lifeworld farther than Socrates had done. In fact Plato started a university, a college, for people to come and study philosophy and other disciplines. He created an institution and framework that challenged tradition and religion and kept the practice of philosophy alive and it has continued into our present.

As for those who were mourning Socrates's fate, he tells them to use reason and not to follow superstition. Do not fear something just because it is unknown. Perhaps death is a good thing. Logically, he says that death is either one of two things: a deep sleep, a sleep so deep you do not even dream, or it is a migration of the soul. There is no need to fear either. If death is the end, then death will feel as it felt before you were born. A sort of nothingness, a sleep so deep you don't dream. If death is not the end, if the soul lives on, then great, start the new adventure; as Socrates puts it, a "good man cannot be harmed either in life or in death."[1]

---
1 Ibid., p. 42.

20

In the *Crito* we get a different Socrates, more mature than the Socrates of the *Euthyphro* in how he talks to Crito. Of course, Crito is his friend and, equal to Socrates, is concerned with truth. Nonetheless Crito is human and is susceptible to worries about his reputation. If Socrates doesn't escape from prison, Crito is afraid that people will think he was too cheap or too afraid to help. Also, it would seem that they let their enemies win, and that Socrates would be abandoning his children. Crito tells Socrates that they can avoid getting in trouble for helping him escape and that Socrates will be happy living somewhere else. Crito, as being a more respectable citizen, is concerned with his reputation, probably is aware of the gossip, and probably has a Facebook page.

Socrates doesn't care what the majority think about him. In Crito's eyes you should be concerned with what the majority thinks, for they can harm you, and in fact they have put Socrates in jail and condemned him to death. Socrates says the majority cannot inflict the greatest harm or the greatest good for they "cannot make a man either wise or foolish, but they inflict things haphazardly."[1] In Socrates's trial he was barely found guilty; with a jury of 501, he only needed 30 more votes to walk away free. But then many of those who voted him innocent turned around and voted to have him killed during the punishment phase. Perhaps Socrates provoked the jury to get the verdict he wanted. Nonetheless, if others can be that easily manipulated, then it proves Socrates right concerning "inflicting things haphazardly."

Socrates teaches a type of objectivity. He wants to know if his actions are good "not only now but at all times." Socrates gets Crito to admit that we should not listen to everyone's opinion, but only some opinions, namely those coming from wise people. He uses the analogy of the body. We should listen to the doctor or the trainer. If we disobey the good opinions, we will harm our bodies. So it is "with actions just and unjust, shameful and beautiful, good and bad." When it comes to the body, life is not worth living when it is ruined, and it is more so with the essentially human part of us, our mind or our soul. Such "that the most important thing is not life, but the good life... And that the good life, the beautiful life, and the just life are the same."

The relevant question to ask, according to Socrates, is whether or not it is just for him to escape from prison when the Athenians have not acquitted him. Socrates is steadfast. He says "one must never in any way do wrong willingly" for "wrongdoing or injustice is in every way harmful and shameful

---

1 All of my quotations in this section from Plato are from *The Trial and Death of Socrates*, pp. 45–9.

to the wrongdoer." It's even wrong to inflict wrong when another has wronged you. When we understand what the just thing is, we must fulfill it in actuality and not cheat on it. To cheat on his punishment is to cheat himself, and is an attempt to destroy the law and the city.

21

One can look at this in relation to Martin Luther King Jr. He was faced with a situation similar to that of Socrates with the difference that, in the case of Socrates, the law was just. Socrates had no problem with a law against corrupting the youth; he just thought he was innocent of the charge. The question, for Socrates, was how to show he was innocent without destroying the law itself. In the case of MLK, the laws were unjust. The segregation laws were unjust. How do you show that a law is wrong while also keeping yourself just and honorable? Civil disobedience was the method he chose. It's a type of determinate negation. By showing up at a restaurant to eat, in other words just doing normal activities, you negate the irrational and unjust law. By negating the common practice of segregation through moral activity, you show the wrong of segregation. You force racists to have to expel you just for sitting down to dinner. You make them absurd. Of course, power and fear, not just goodness and love, often are also needed. This is where, perhaps, Malcolm X comes in handy.

22

In any case, the way Socrates sees it: we owe the city much, from bringing one to birth at the hospital or by the midwife, to marrying the parents, to providing education and jobs, security, arts, physical fitness, and culture. In this way we owe our country more than our parents, for even our parents' life is dependent on the city. If we don't like something we must obey or change it; "one must obey the commands of one's city and country or persuade it as to the nature of justice."[1] Socrates has never left the city, except for military service, and so has a tacit contract to obey even when things don't go his way. There is a difference between a good law applied incorrectly and a bad law that needs to be changed. This is where logical reasoning, moral reasoning, and persuasion come together. Socrates will not engage in a practice he finds wrong; he will not attempt to escape, for his actions and thoughts form a harmonious unity.

And despite Socrates saying that Crito's initial reasons are not important, he addresses them at the end of the dialogue. Crito is his friend. Crito is one

1 Ibid., p. 51.

who matters. In the heart of the dialogue Socrates articulates his philosophical reasons that Crito respects but might not completely understand or accept. Still, Socrates wants Crito to understand on Crito's own terms, too. Socrates does not forget what Crito said early in the dialogue and he addresses Crito's more common concerns at the end. By articulating reasons not to escape in a way that Crito will be sure to understand, Socrates does an act of justice toward his good friend. Socrates tells Crito he fears Crito will be in danger if he helps Socrates escape. Crito could be exiled, disenfranchised, or lose property because of it. In a new place, Socrates would arrive as a criminal, an enemy of the state, and wouldn't be taken seriously. People will be more interested in hearing the story of how he escaped than they will be in engaging in his philosophy. Socrates won't be able to go to any civilized place. (He could end up isolated, like Snowden.) And his children will be better off if they stay in Athens as innocent victims. His children are citizens of Athens and Socrates's friends can look after them there; Socrates knows Crito will take care of his sons in Athens.

23

Today we talk a lot about taking care of the youth. Yet we spank our children, and let many go hungry; daycare is too expensive; we leave our children to watch hours and hours of television; we damage their brains by putting them in MMA and football; we buy them violent videos games; and we make high school a torture for most kids. Then after we dull young people throughout high school, we let the military come into the schools and feed them the lie of a glorious military life. Many youth who go straight into the military suffer from lack of success and lack of opportunity. Going into the service is a way to secure one's material base and gain some recognition. Yet the hyper-celebration some families display when their son or daughter joins up exposes the lie. Pretending we are not engaged in unjust wars, we throw the sticker "my son fights for your freedom" on the car's bumper. Of course, America's wars and military adventures are not about freedom. The military industrial complex is corrupting our youth and we are all to blame for this. And let's be clear: your son and daughter are not fighting for my freedom. And let's be honest: we all collectively messed up, and that's why the lost youth are in the military. No one dreams of going straight into the military after high school. That's not the American dream. Saying this is harsh, but this is the Socratic way.

24

The story of Socrates in the early Platonic dialogues focuses on the cultivation of a robust internal self interacting rationally with the external world. By staying pure, and not trying to escape, Socrates will have lived a harmonious life of reflective action, a philosophical life. He will stay true to the self he created and to his society that allowed him to become himself. Also, he will be better positioned just in case Hades does exist. Yet Socrates is not an atomistic individualist. He is not only focused on himself. In fact Socrates puts his loyalty to his friends above any gods or abstract principles or dogma, and even above his own life. He is worried about Crito's beliefs insofar as they can lead to actions that harm Crito, and insofar as they make Crito intrinsically suffer. Crito is too concerned about his reputation. He believes that reputation is important and his actions are driven by a desire to secure a good reputation in society. According to Socrates acting in order to please some anonymous people is destructive to an individual. Socrates is concerned with those who matter, those who understand him. Socrates doesn't just try to change Crito's beliefs, he also, and more importantly, tries to change Crito's actions. He basically is putting Crito in charge of his children after he dies, and he gives Crito a symbolic errand to perform after he dies. It's a religious offering that Crito may have needed, although Socrates did not. Socrates's actions then improve Crito, and Crito's future actions will not be corrupted by menacing beliefs.

25

The death scene of the *Phaedo* is a moving account of Socrates's final moments. Preceding this scene Socrates gives a fantastic account of what Hades or the afterworld might be like. He admits that it's not sensible but he thinks the vision, the aesthetic portrait, is a noble one. It's a type of aesthetically-driven Pascalian wager, not motivated by fear of death or punishment but invented to promote a life of beauty, morality, and internal success. When one truly understands what's important, dreaming of a beautiful future does not risk the present, for the present is lived reflectively and honestly. According to Socrates, the real risk is not whether you believe in gods or not, rather it is the risk of wasting one's life. We waste our lives if we do not act virtuously towards other human beings and toward ourselves.

Socrates understood that the goal is not to transcend to another realm, and if there is another realm the reward is simply more of Socrates's same life. And if there is nothing after death, he has lost nothing because he has always been himself. He has lived the life he chose, based not on superstition but on reason and concern for real others. It is a rewarding life, a virtuous life that advocates consciousness, virtuous acts, and promotes meaning, stability, and happiness. If the soul is immortal, and if he spent his time on the pleasure of learning "and adorned his soul not with alien but with its own ornaments, namely moderation, righteousness, courage, freedom, and truth,"[1] he will be positioned for the afterlife. Intrinsically his life will be good, and instrumentally he is ready for whatever comes next.

26

Socrates takes his bath so that the women don't have to bathe him after he dies, and he tells Crito and his other friends that he doesn't need to tell them anything new, just take "good care of your own selves in whatever you do."[2] He has no concern for how he is buried. His body, without consciousness, a body that is not reflectively acting, is not him. And be careful during the funeral to not confuse the body with Socrates, for "to express oneself badly is not only faulty as far as the language goes, but does some harm to the soul. You must be of good cheer, and say you are burying my body, and bury it in any way you like and think most customary."

His last words are to Crito and he says, "Crito, we owe a cock to Asclepius; make this offering to him and do not forget." Perhaps Socrates, as Nietzsche argued, does think that death is the cure for what we suffer in life, or perhaps Foucault was on to something when he said we should translate the "we" as "you," in reference to Crito. Perhaps Socrates was referring to Crito being cured of his obsession with his reputation, and Socrates's last act was a noble one serving his friend. Perhaps it meant something else. Perhaps it never happened, and Plato made it up. What a story. Any of the interpretations can produce a wonderful narrative, an inspirational story, or even a cruddy one if we are not careful. There is no one true story here, as Socrates's life, like each of our lives, is not a story. We can make anything into a story, but nothing can make our lives a story, for you and I are real and living lives that will unfold contingently and unpredictably. Only after the fact can we choose to interpret our actions as a story.

27

Hegel and Nietzsche were the modern philosophers who gave rise to the idea that life is historical and interpretive. They indirectly promoted the idea

---

1 Ibid., p. 55.
2 All of my quotations in this section from Plato are from *The Trial and Death of Socrates*, pp. 55–58.

of life as a story. But they brought these points out not because they thought life was a story, but to counter ahistorical and absolutist metaphysical and epistemological philosophies. They challenged the idea of a thing-in-itself and the idea that underneath all our experiences there is some substratum that escapes us, as well as the idea of a "true" self underlying our actions. The metaphor of life as a story was just meant to highlight that we are the sum of our actions and effects in the world. A character in a novel is nothing but what's written in the text, and our lives are nothing but how we have "written" our lives. At some point modern theorists forgot this and started literally thinking of life as a story, and began believing it means more than it does. This is unfortunate because it eclipses the deeper points that Socrates, Hegel, and Nietzsche were making.

Against the idea of an unchanging and universal human nature Hegel emphasizes the social and historical construction of our lives. Nietzsche attacked the idea of a "True World" against which everything else was mere appearance. As Nietzsche showed, when the so-called true world dissolves, so does the so-called apparent world. He replaced abstract Truth with contextual truth. Ironically the dialectic has unfolded so that these insights have been pushed into an absurd conclusion that life IS a story. Socrates didn't think of his life as a story; he saw that human life was about "knowing thyself," through reflective and virtuous action, not through a narrative. As such he simply tried to make himself and those who matter proud. When people conceive of their lives as stories they tell stories, to themselves and others. They rewrite history and try to control the narrative, while acting in ways to fit the story they are selling. They become slaves to the narrative or ignore aspects of themselves that don't fit the narrative. In this way those who see human life as a story unwittingly fall victim to a false dialectic that refutes itself as "life as a story" congeals into a metaphysical claim.

Fortunately, we can push back against this silliness. Stories are but ideas and accounts looking for coherence; they are not actions; they don't have to materially connect to reality; they are abstract; they are ideological. They are not life. Lahiri makes this point eloquently when talking about writing novels. "Even a novel drawn from reality, faithful to it, is not the truth, just as the image in the mirror is not a person in flesh and blood. It remains, that is, an abstraction, no matter how realistic, how close to the facts."[1] Life is not the story that we tell ourselves; rather, life is the practices and actions we engage in. Life is a practical, material creation. When we transcend the myth of story, we start to create ourselves. When we consciously and reflectively act, we become more than ourselves; and it is here that the idea

---

1 Jhumpa Lahiri, *In Other Words*, p. 227.

of narrative makes sense, and may even guide us. Stories can help to guide us, help us to make sense of our lives, and help to connect that sense to others, to community. All ideologies have these features. They rationalize, reflect, distort, and offer promise. They do not get to the *is* of life. Still, the more we plan and reflect, and act accordingly, the more mature, which is to say more human, we can become. In this way we will get closer to Socrates and farther from gods and reactionary atheism. As we get closer to Socrates we stop being corrupted, and we begin to make ourselves and those who matter proud.

Chapter 3. Descartes's Joke

1

Many people today think we are living in a kind of dark age, and some believe we are living in end times. Humans seem to have a need to be driven by hope or fear, but fear is often the drug of choice. Everyone prefers to feel special; and yearning to witness, or at least contemplate, the destruction of humanity, apparently makes a lot of people feel warm and fuzzy inside. What else explains the willful ignorance of those who claim to know about the apocalypse, or those who think they have decoded some eschatology to the exact date? These prophets were in abundance before the year 1000, for the Bible loves that number, and lots of God folk put their chips down on that date. Failure doesn't seem to affect these types. The year 2000 was still defendable as the end date, not as sexy as 1000, but double the fun in a world as profane as ours. 2012 was just pathetic, though.

The rest of us, not so saturated with *Thanatos*, we can contemplate hope. Socrates is still a model here because his version of hope carried a seemingly doable notion of change. Hope and change, for Socrates, weren't explicitly political; they focused on inward success, excellence, virtue, and truth — for the happy few. Still, the Christian mind latched on to these values and re-conceptualized them, aped them, for the obedient and fearful masses.

2

Socrates had unique answers for at least two fundamental questions: What counts as a successful life, and why be moral? Unlike many, who then as now, believe that success is defined by material gain and external rewards, Socrates stressed inner success and a life of virtue. Success, according to Socrates, is living in harmony with higher principles, doing what's just, and adhering to truth. But in a polytheistic world, where the gods didn't seem to agree with Socrates, or care about him, it's not surprising that his viewpoint did not carry the day. Many shrugged him off — why listen to a loser like Socrates when those who are successful in life, and even the gods, are breaking the rules and taking what they want?

But when people start believing in a perfect God, a God who is omniscient, omnipotent, and omnibenevolent, these fundamental puzzles are pushed into a coherent and objective direction and toward an absolute solution. Ironically, they are partly pushed in a Socratic direction. Under the tutelage of a perfect God, success is defined by what this God says it is, by God's higher principles, by God's truth. Success is determined, ultimately, by whether one ends up in heaven or not. Morality means following God's commandments, doing what God commands. With God as superior, the questions of success and morality transcend the human dimension. One could escape judgment in our world but still never escape the gaze of God. God sees all, God judges, and God decides whether your life was successful and ethical. God, as George W. Bush said about himself, is the decider.

3

Philosophy and theology have danced a dialectical dance for a long time, beginning even before Plato had Socrates and Euthyphro battle it out. Of course, as we know, Socrates clearly won that battle, but in the medieval age philosophy lost the war. Philosophy came to be of service to theology, but could not officially challenge theology. God could not seriously be confronted. To do philosophy was to assume God, to start from God. In this way theology was bigger than philosophy, and it tried to colonize the whole world. It put culture, the state, and the economy under its tutelage, and blended them all in an undifferentiated muddy soup. It justified this paltry meal on two fronts: revealed and natural theology. It became totalitarian. Revealed and natural theology weaved together when necessary and useful, and they stood independently if and when they desired. It was a vicious cycle, comparable to Penelope's weaving a burial shroud and then unraveling it every night. Philosophy was close to death; it was close to drowning in the 'sea of the supernatural. If Penelope had ever finished the shroud, her marriage to Odysseus would have been over, and if theology could ever weave itself a discipline without philosophy, philosophy would have died. But theology is make-believe; it unravels itself, its unphilosophical shroud was never finished.

In any case, natural theology used the tools of philosophy and science, logic and experience, the *a priori* and the *a posteriori*, to uncover or justify the holy universe. Revealed theology got to be more adventurous and mythical. It could sidestep philosophical arguments and scientific method for the pleasure of the idiosyncratic, the hope of faith, the dream of intuition, the excitement of esoteric and sacred texts, and the lust for prophets. For too long during this time, philosophy played a maidservant to the theological juggernaut but, at some point, even Christian minds, or at least a few bright Christian minds, felt trapped in God's torture chamber. The critique of theology was internal, and Thomas Aquinas, being fat and phat, split, like he would a wild boar, philosophy and theology again.

4

One day we might discover the God gene. Some have claimed it exists, but at this point it is just an intriguing fantasy of the atheism–scientism crowd. It could reduce religious people to a genetic disorder. If you are religious, you might just need a cure, or you might get sympathy for your handicap, and you might test your children to see if they are afflicted. Perhaps you abort if your fetus has it. Or, perhaps, the idea of a God gene could turn against those who don't have it. What if God gave some the gene and others God didn't? Could we have a high-tech solution to the problem of predestination? Just get your genes tested. Besides finding out that you come from a bunch of places and races you never realized before, you also find out if you are one of the chosen.

Descartes anticipated this. Descartes claimed that those who look inside themselves and cannot find God simply are not looking carefully or hard enough. He goes so far as to claim that one is accountable for it if one cannot intuit God and the soul. As Descartes puts it, "Those without this knowledge are blameworthy."[1] Clearly this is a joke, and we can have fun trying to find God by taking a journey into our complicated, neurotic selves.

5

The Ontological Argument claims we can find God just by analyzing the concepts in our head; just study your language and God will speak to you. This argument aims to be purely logical and rational. It tries to get to God without looking at the world or at experience. It is a model for an *a priori* argument. It has many formulations, but Descartes prefers the term "perfection" (Aquinas used "greatest possible being") and we will follow the

---

1 Descartes, *Meditations on First Philosophy*, p. 1.

sickly Frenchman's lead. The argument basically goes: God is by definition perfect. It is more perfect to exist than not to exist. Therefore God must exist.

This argument is a bit slipperier (more perfectly slipperier?) than it might first seem. It appears to be begging the question but it really is not, since the conclusion is not in the premises. But both premises are debatable. One could define God as perfect but one need not. Further, defining God is to define a concept, and concepts don't exist independently of agents to define or to conceptualize them. This implies we are more necessary than God, if God is to exist. And, if so, could God really be perfect? In Aquinas's vernacular assertion that "God is the greatest possible being," we still run into problems since two Gods (although not logically coherent) would be greater. And defining someone as perfect or greatest just because he or she knows everything, can do everything, and happens to be perfectly good is only one way of defining perfection. Someone with those attributes or qualities might just be annoying and not so perfect. Nobody likes a know-it-all. In fact, when we meet people who, so to speak, know it all and can do it all, we don't think of them as perfect, we think of them as tiresome. Power and lack of contingency do not equal perfection, rather it kind of makes you pity this poor God creature, who must live endlessly with nothing to look forward to, no surprises, no new experiences, nothing new. With God it's all "been there, done that."

The second premise (it is more perfect to exist than not to exist) is a value judgment that is often considered true. Most of us prefer to exist, and we think that things, especially good things, are better when they actually exist. But to say that it's more perfect to exist is pushing it; I can think of a few things that would be more perfect if they didn't exist. I might even think God would be more perfect if God didn't exist. Just the idea of God might be more perfect and beautiful than any existing God. Aren't many of our dreams better, more perfect, than our realities? Do you have to always have something, literally possess it, own it, to consider it superior? Further, saying that God is more perfect if God exists is especially problematic because perfection and existence are not straightforward. As we saw in the last chapter, existence or being seems to also include nothing. And what is perfection anyway? The problem here is that, conceptually speaking, God and God's perfection are just ideas we have invented. And the meaning of perfection changes its meaning depending on the object one is applying it to. Martin Luther King Jr.'s existence is more perfect than his nonexistence, but the Black Death's nonexistence would have been more perfect than its existence. Then, even concerning the object (or concept) at hand — God —

as said above, it's not clear that God's existence would be more perfect. More perfect for whom or from what perspective?

In any case, any argument that attempts to discover and prove God, or the opposite, through definitional logic or pure reasoning alone will not do. The idea that by defining a concept and then concluding that by virtue of this definition of the concept something about the world is objectively true cannot work. Theory must be proved in reality. The idea of a theory outside us, a theory that need not be proved in reality, or in practice, is incoherent or empty. In either case the theory or idea is false. In fact this is what makes a theory or idea false.

It's even more complicated because concepts come through us, and we can never shed our skins to analyze the concept outside of the creative, human building of it; there is no way to bridge the dualism. There is no way to test for something completely outside us. In fact if it is completely outside us, we could not experience it. This is not because we are inadequate; rather it is because this supposedly existing thing isn't real. The dualism is a fiction. Arguments of this kind presuppose a dualism, an inner and an outer, a human and an essentially nonhuman realm. What would this God so different from us be? This God is perfect, infinite, everywhere and nowhere, and yet we can grasp it but not grasp it. If we can grasp it, then we can challenge it; if we cannot grasp it then we are wasting our time. But as soon as someone says you cannot grasp it he or she has conceded you can. Unless they are speaking nonsense we are talking about it, and to talk about it is to, at least partly, grasp it. This is what is meant by saying that there is no getting to an object itself without us to help construct it. Any concept or object we bring up, or contemplate through consciousness, is necessarily and inevitably linked to us. We cannot get outside ourselves or get to the concept or object without us. In this sense it is circular. The object or concept's truth value cannot be tested without our contribution to its being, and so there is no clean sense of what it would be without us. Do cats dream of an Über-cat God and do dogs fantasize about The Big Dog upstairs? God, as autonomous, would require the ability to speak to us without going through us, and that is impossible from the start. Nietzsche's quip, "Is man only God's mistake or God only man's mistake?"[1] must be answered as the latter, then. But nobody enjoys admitting their mistakes. God is a big idea, yet one that relies on us, and perhaps we rely on it to move the dialectic forward. The dialectic moves forward first through the mistake of treating "existence" as any other predicate, as if it were tantamount to omnipotence and omniscience. This mistake is required for the Ontological Argument to be intelligible at all. But then this move sets the terms and the limits of its validity, which, of course,

---

1 Nietzsche, *Twilight of the Idols*, p. 33.

turns out to be its invalidity. God is invalid, yet God needs us, and do we really want to discard something that needs us? Or perhaps we need God. God is our mistake, and if it's true that our mistakes make us who we are as much as anything else, then it might not be a mistake to say, "Thank you, Jesus."

6

Where the Ontological Argument was medieval enough to take the definition of the concept of God as self-evident, and so was a perfect fantasy, the Cosmological Argument even caused Stephen Hawking[1] to address it. The Cosmological Argument uses both *a priori* and *a posteriori* reasoning. Many people will agree that, speaking logically, either the universe has always existed or it came into being at some point. Experience though tells us that all things have a cause; the world works by cause and effect. Therefore the universe must have had a cause. Well, what could "cause" a universe? Only God could cause a universe, and since the universe exists, God must exist. Someone might ask, "Well, if every event has a cause, what caused God?" We could bicker over whether a supernatural being is essentially different and non-material, etc., and so is outside the logic of "every event has a cause," but I prefer to think that God's mom caused God. Perhaps his dad played a small role, yet surely God's dad was more absent than God is toward us. We really shouldn't blame God for not ever showing up. We know these things run in families. If your dad is a drunk, you will probably be a drunk. If your dad was absent, you will probably be absent; or you will overcompensate and become a helicopter parent. So maybe we got off lucky with a deadbeat God. But it would have been cool if God were more of a Disneyland dad.

Hawking argues that some things in the universe can self-cause, and the universe could and can self-cause, so we don't have to posit something outside the universe to explain the universe's existence. If the universe can self-cause, or self-create, it wouldn't need an agent or an outside force to bring it into being. And if space and time are intimately connected, perhaps as space decreases, time does too. When there is no time, there is also no space, with no space there is no universe; and yet it could self-create, in sync with time, without God. In other words, God is not necessary to explain space, time, or the universe, so the Cosmological Argument falls apart. But this is unfortunate because it takes the bite out of St. Augustine's response to the question, "What was God doing before God created the universe?" His response was, "creating Hell in which to put people who asked that

---

1 See Stephen Hawking, *The Grand Design*.

question." If we don't have space without time, then perhaps we wouldn't have God either. One could counter that God is outside space and time and the universe, but that is just empty theory. If God is outside space and time God needs to get his act together. God wouldn't be without a world, and the world doesn't need God to be. Rather, as space and time are formed, so is God. In one sense then the universe creates God. And this one sense is the true sense. We did create God and have hell to pay for it.

7

The argument for God's existence that seems to speak to most people today is the Teleological Argument (also called The Argument by Design). It goes something like this. Things such as watches, ships, and cars display order and design and have intelligent creators. The universe displays order and design. Therefore the universe had an intelligent creator. There's a lot one can do to make this argument have more teeth to it, especially by talking about order and design on both a micro and macro level. For example, it's popular to cite the sophistication and complexity of the human eye and the orbit of the planets. Most people making these arguments are wearing glasses and probably know that the orbit of the planets is not mysterious; nonetheless that doesn't seem to stop them. And, of course, one can, and many have, questioned the notions of order and especially design when it comes to the world and humans' place in it. Further, it doesn't get you anywhere close to a perfect being as creator. Still, it's an argument by analogy which has some intuitive plausibility. But if God wanted us to believe, why not just talk to us as a parent, a superior, or even a friend? You don't take a kid and give the child life, and then hide, and then indirectly say, "I'm here in the corner, worship and honor me." It's just bizarre that today people would turn to a supernatural explanation to get a sense of our world. With the amazing advances in science, the incredible knowledge in physics, chemistry, and biology, why settle for some crusty myth about an old dude with a beard? That's like having access to all the wonderful 18th- and 19th-century Russian, French, and American literature at your disposal and then picking up a contemporary romance novel instead. Actually that's what most people do. They prefer *Fifty Shades of Gray* to *A Harlot High and Low*. Or maybe it's just laziness, since scientific knowledge does take some work, and some math skills, and we all know about the average American and math. Whatever it is (and it is the metaphysical urge, actually), it does show the power of human denial and willful ignorance. In the end then, the argument by design tells us more about our design than anything else.

8

The problem of evil is still probably the biggest threat questioning the logic of believing in the idea of a perfect God. The Ancient Greeks did not box themselves into a corner when it came to the supernatural. They believed in so many gods and so many levels, including fate, that it was easy to link the supernatural with actual existing reality. But when we decided that God was perfect — God is all-powerful, all-good, and all-knowing — we constructed a deductive puzzle, a closed argument against God's existence, whether we realize it or not. The argument goes: If God is all-powerful, God could prevent evil. And if God is all-knowing, God would know how to prevent evil. And if God is all-good, God would want to prevent evil. But there is evil. Therefore God, conceived as a perfect being, must be a fiction, or God doesn't exist, or better yet, God is not all that.

People often miss the strength of this argument because they don't realize the argument is talking about a narrow part of human experience. Evil is rare, although it gets a lot of attention, for obvious reasons. People can deny the premise that there is evil in the world, but rather than this seeming plausible, it just sounds as if they don't want to take on the challenge of this argument. In any case, when theists try to dismiss the problem of evil they often invoke the "free will" defense and say that God didn't want to create robots, so God gave us free will and had to allow for evil. The beauty of the free will defense is that it covers all instances of evil. When people abuse their free will, they are responsible for the evil they commit, and Satan, when he abuses his angel-like free will, is responsible for natural disasters. This explains away evil with one clean term: free will. The first obvious problem, though, is that it forces one to concede that God is not all-powerful or all-knowing. For it is saying the God was not strong enough, or smart enough, or clever enough, or creative enough, to create a world without evil and with free will.

And in fact it makes God an idiot. Evil seems not to be very important when it comes to most willful actions. Evil doesn't play a role in much of our day-to-day lives, and it's easy to judge someone's worth outside of whether that person actually committed evil acts or not. No normal person gets up in the morning and says, "Thank you God for giving me free will, now I can kill someone; it makes me feel so free and so alive!" No, in almost all our actions, thoughts, and beliefs, evil does not play a role, so to think you would be a robot if you were not allowed to experience or commit evil is silly. The problem of evil starts before anyone does something evil. The problem of evil asks why we even have the potential for evil. Why would God put the potential in us, and how could God put it in us, if God is all-good? And then why do we think we wouldn't be free if we couldn't commit evil acts.

Without evil there is still a wide range of things a human being can do. Does the fact that we cannot fly like Superman mean we are not free? Does the fact that we cannot will others dead with our thought mean we are not free? Does the fact that we are born with only two legs, while horses have four legs, mean we are not fast? Is Usain Bolt prevented from running fast, from exercising free will, because he is limited to two legs? If I could only be really bad, but not evil, would I really be prevented from acting freely? And, by the way, was there evil before the fall and will there be evil in heaven? If you answer no to either of these, then do you think that heaven is a place crammed with robots?

If you really think about it, the term "free will" is misleading. We don't have free will. We cannot do freely what we will. If we could, I would be dunking a basketball right now, you might be flying, someone else might be willing her enemy dead (and he would die), another might be willing himself good at calculus. Kobe surely would be better at basketball right now, in 2016, if it was about will. The truth is that some things we can will into existence and some we can't. We can do some things and some things we cannot do. Presumably if angels exist they would have greater free will than we do. But then, what does this say about free will? If one can have more or less of it (like angels having more), then it makes no sense to claim humans have free will. If it were possible for us to have more, then it's not free yet, and you are admitting that God divvies up free will and parcels it out in different quantities. You are also admitting that God could have given us less of it. And if God can do that, then God must explain why it makes sense to allow for evil. Why not spread our will around so we have healthy and complex choices but cannot be evil jerks? But if there are not different quantities of free will, if you either have it or don't, then evil still needs to be explained. In others words if God gave us free will, we would always have it; we would be free regardless of whether evil existed or not and regardless of whether we could commit evil acts. It would be an internal state not dependent on actualization. If we have it internally, it cannot be contingent on evil, or anything external; free will would be a state of being regardless of external possibilities. Free will, if it were something set, would be comparable to being pregnant. You can't be more pregnant. You are either pregnant or not. You either have free will or not. Saying there needs to be evil for me to have free will is like saying one can be more pregnant or less pregnant depending on what's going on in the world outside the pregnant woman.

In any case, what we do know is that there are limits on what we can do, what we can think, and what we can will. Why would a God allow for evil? Wouldn't it have been enough for God to see us act very badly in order for God to know we are bad? How does the presence of evil help determine if one is worthy of Heaven? It's like a college instructor grading students. A student who gets all the answers incorrect is easy to grade. Instructors can tell right away that that person should not pass. One need not read the whole exam if the first half is plagiarized, completely incorrect, or blank. It's the exams that are borderline that require analysis. Evil is not borderline. One need not be able to commit evil to avoid being a robot, to have robust free will. And if free will is so important, should all the individuals on earth be given an opportunity to exercise their free will? But the fact that many people die very young refutes the notion that free will is central to the test. Unless you take the extreme position, like St. Augustine, who thought that he was being selfish for greedily sucking on his mom's breast as a baby,[1] you probably can see that most people throughout history have exercised very little free will. In fact, far too many people die before they even reach ten years old. How can we reconcile ourselves to the idea that evil is necessary in order to allow for free will when free will is not central to the human experience?

At this point some will say symmetry matters. For us to experience the highest goods, we must be capable of the basest actions. First, this is acknowledging that God is not perfect or the greatest. It makes God subject to the laws of symmetry, and hence below them. And, of course, symmetry isn't necessary. The universe clearly is not balanced, justice and injustice do not even out, and God can do anything, so could not be subject to the laws of symmetry even if these laws did in fact exist. Even little kids understand when something is good regardless of whether they understand evil yet. We don't have to tell our children horror stories the night before Christmas so they can really enjoy Christmas the next day. Clearly, having evil in our world does not make us appreciate the good. In fact, finding out about evil, or experiencing evil, or knowing people you care about who have suffered evil, often prevents us from appreciating the good. Evil scars many for life and tortures them until they die.

9

The second popular defense is the Big Picture defense. It's true our lives are but a flicker within human history, and the universe's history, and perhaps God's history. Maybe in the big picture what we take for evil will turn out not to be evil. What we take as evil, when seen as part of the big picture, could turn out to be good. It would be like a scene early in a film that turns out not to be what we thought it was. We might watch the beginning of a movie and hate a character or see an action that we are sure is evil, but as the film unfolds we begin to like the character, we see her virtue, and

---

1 See *The Confessions*, Book I.

we realize the event we took to be evil was not evil at all. In fact it might have been good, just, and ethical. St. Augustine compared the judgment that something was evil to someone looking at a small splat of paint on a huge canvas and judging the artwork by the splat alone. Seeing only the splat and not the whole piece makes us incompetent to judge.

Another popular analogy is to imagine being taken to the dentist as a small child. One might interpret the event as evil. The child may think her mother has handed her over to some stranger who brought her into a small, scary room, strapped her to a chair, opened her mouth and tortured her. But in the big picture, when she's older, she realizes that mom's action was one of kindness. Mom wanted her to have healthy, attractive teeth, and now she has healthy, attractive teeth, a winning smile, and the world smiles back at her. Of course, we could get really existential and extend it out further to the day she gets really old, and no matter how much care she takes, her teeth will rot, turn yellow, and fall out. She may come to hate her mother and regret ever being born. Most senior citizens have lots of dental issues, and we haven't even mentioned vision, hearing, blood pressure, cholesterol, knees, hips, and so on. Perhaps, in the big picture, what we take for evil will not seem as evil a little later, and then in the bigger picture we may see that it was even more evil than we could have ever imagined. Still, as an analogy, the big picture defense has some plausibility, but God clearly has a lot of explaining to do. But given that God has eternity to convince us that genocide is not evil, we cannot rule it out 100%. The big picture defense really shows that in the big picture we want a happy ending despite, or perhaps because of, the way we know reality actually works. Even if it doesn't work as an argument against the problem of evil, it does make one feel decent about human beings. Despite the evidence, most people believe that goodness, justice, and beauty will win in the end. These people have never heard of the New England Patriots.

10

Finally we have the anti-anthropomorphic defense. Perhaps God is so unlike us that to attribute human understanding of concepts to God is futile. God is a supreme being, perfect, infinite, and so on, so God wouldn't be limited to a human interpretation of concepts including evil. In other words, what we take as evil might not really get to what evil is for a being such as God. To judge God by our human categories is unfair, or a category mistake. This has some logic to it, because if there were a God who created the whole universe, this God would have to have an incredibly complex, superior, or essentially different nature than ours. This being would be working on a completely different level. But one could still ask why this perfect God can't get us to understand God's version of evil. It also leaves us to wonder if God doesn't love as we do. If we are working with different definitions of evil, then perhaps we are working with different definitions of love. In that case, God doesn't love you in the way you were taught God does. This makes the idea of a caring God, a God with a plan, a God trying to test faith, and so on, off the table. This God sounds more like the God of deism; it sounds as if we are the mice on the ship in Voltaire's *Candide*. As such the anti-anthropomorphic defense has sailed to a place it didn't intend. But like Columbus, the truth of the destination will probably not be admitted by the religious explorer, and the natives will be the ones that suffer.

11

A version of Pascal's Wager can be useful for showing how lots of people think about religion today. Many will say things such as, "You don't want to take any chances, for if God exists, it's better to be safe than sorry." The idea here is that it's safer to believe in God just in case there is a God. One doesn't want to miss out on heaven or go to hell. Pascal just gives structure to this reasoning. He gives the idea form by exploiting the dialectic between theory and practice. In fact, he is on to something important when he distinguishes between theory and practice, because this distinction is central to capturing the inadequacy of belief. Starting with belief we can say that the Western mind easily posits that we have three options. One can believe in God, not believe in God, or be unsure — one can be theist, atheist, or agnostic. Of course we could posit more options but the wager pretty much assumes these three, and for our purposes this is fine. Yet even if we can theoretically imagine at least three options, in practice we have only two options. We can either live for God or live against God, so to speak. In practice we are actually theist or atheist depending on how we live, depending on our actions.

Then how should we live? If in practice we only have two options, we might ask which option is consistent with truth. But to answer this we would have to know whether God exists or not. But when thinking about the God question Pascal does not think we can know. He asserts that evidence cannot solve the God puzzle. His poetic phrase in *The Pensées* is, "If there is a God, He is infinitely incomprehensible, since, having neither parts nor limits, He has no affinity to us. We are then incapable of knowing either what He is or if He is." The implication here is that there is no evidence concerning God's existence. What one person sees as evidence, another will explain without God. What one person sees as evidence against God, another will explain with God. Pascal seemed to understand that belief and desire drives how we interpret the world and there is no shutting down belief and desire to get to the truth about God's existence. Rather than looking at which belief is more likely, or more rational, based on evidence, Pascal asks what is the payoff or potential payoff, for either betting on God or not betting on God. There are two possible outcomes: winning or losing. If you bet on God, it means you start living the life of a theist, you start living the life of a believer. If God exists, then you win the bet, meaning that when you die you get to go to heaven. On the other hand, if you bet on God but there is no God, you will have lost. If there is no God, then you have spent your life talking to and worshiping something that doesn't exist. Besides looking really silly, if you could look back, you would have to admit you wasted the chance to live your life truly, authentically, and as you really would have wanted to. You missed your only opportunity to be authentic and develop yourself your way with your pleasures, dreams, and desires; you missed your opportunity to become actualized. You lived as a sort of brainwashed person.

Betting against God also means winning or losing. If you bet against God and live this so-called authentic life, and there is no God, then you've put your chips down on the right horse and should have no regrets. But if God exists then you go to hell. According to Pascal, the rational option is to bet on God. The chance for an infinite jackpot or infinite suffering versus the lifespan of a human being is too big to ignore. The chance for an infinite reward or punishment is essentially greater than any finite reward or punishment, so mathematically it makes sense. Considered from a strategic or instrumental angle, it also makes sense. As an abstraction it makes sense. But our lives are concrete and finite. Do we really even know what's at stake in the wager when we cannot really understand living forever or being infinite? Do we really know what's at stake in this bet? Of course, mathematical reasoning points toward choosing God, for mathematical reasoning, like the concept God, lives in the house of theory. Neither one shows up in practice, so we can say, almost by nature, both are ideological. It's never wise to bet on something solely based on an ideology. Contemplating one's life, and its worth, requires thinking about actual practices and concrete actions in this world. Simply determining a life choice based on quantitative factors will not and cannot capture qualitative things such as the meaning of one's existence and the value of one's world. Making one's life meaningful is not a quantitative exercise. Life's value is not in its endurance.

12

If this is the case then Pascal's Wager may have more in common with such things as the phenomenon where people buy massive amounts of lottery tickets, go into a lotto frenzy, when the jackpot gets really high. It just seems to make more sense to get a ticket when $100 million is at stake. But is it really? Living your life hoping for an infinite jackpot might not be living. And can people today really convince themselves to believe in a place called hell that tortures people forever?

Ludwig Feuerbach would argue that if there is no evidence for God, then you should bet against God and seize the living entity within you. The thinking here is to avoid wasting one's life on a conjecture. As with the lottery, rather than buying tickets with the hope of getting rich, live your life in a way so you get rich, or better yet quit obsessing about riches. Rather than spending the present living for a future hope, rather than making choices because you hope to get into heaven one day, Feuerbach would suggest you simply live in the present the right way and make choices because they are the right choices for you and for those who matter. Don't live out of fear or childish hope. What happens after we die no one knows, but we all know, or should know, that we are alive now. According to Feuerbach, a bird in the hand is better than two in the bush, especially if the bush is burning. You know you are alive and have a life (I hope you have a life), and you would like to live it, so don't waste it based on some medieval belief system. It's been said that lottery tickets are a tax on people who are poor at math, and we might say that betting on God is a tax for people who are poor at life. It's one thing to burn a dollar buying a lotto ticket but another thing altogether to burn a life betting on God.

13

Descartes lived during a time when science and religion were explicitly at odds. As a Renaissance man (literally), Descartes drew from the ancients as well as the Middle Ages, yet he developed something new. He wrote the *Meditations* to solve the science/religion debate, and he dedicated it to the Church to protect himself. He even wrote it in Latin rather than French to prove his loyalty. He went so far as to say that those not able to find God within themselves have only themselves to blame. He claimed that he would prove the existence of the soul and God's existence.

Descartes is important when talking about dialectics because, despite what he says in his Preface, he is a modest thinker. Descartes is skeptical even as he attacks skepticism. He is self-reflective and shows that one can treat himself as a distinct interlocutor. Socrates was an extrovert and engaged others to find truth. Descartes proves himself modern by being able to accomplish the same thing, have the same effect, through a dialogue in his mind. He calls his work *Meditations on First Philosophy*. This is meant to signal a metaphysical project, but it is as much a work in epistemology as it is in metaphysics. He dialectically links metaphysics and epistemology, and in so doing points us beyond the dualisms of theory/practice, subject/object, and God/no-God. He writes a series of six meditations and we can see, through the form and content, his dialectical method and his attempt to transcend both God and atheism.

His meditations are not what we might think of when we hear the word meditation today. Descartes does not have a mantra; he doesn't try to clear his mind as a mediator might; but he does try to focus his mind in order to think deeply. Descartes's method of meditation is to use philosophy, reason, and the conscious self to guide him to truth. We can imagine Descartes going to bed and thinking about the puzzle he wants to solve; we can picture him dreaming about it and then envision him waking up and continuing the self-dialogue until he is able to write intelligibly about it. His method is systematic, serious, reflective, and open.

14

Descartes begins Meditation One by acknowledging that in his youth he believed many things that now he knows are false. We have all experienced this; little things from Santa Claus to the tooth fairy, to bigger things such as the infallibility of our parents and the naïve goodness of our nation. Descartes's situation is exacerbated by the fact that he is living in a time of cultural crisis. The authority figures of his time, the Church, taught him that the sun rotates around the earth. The Church grounded the geocentric model in scripture. Although unstated, Descartes probably read many things in the Bible that he knew were false. From moral issues including slavery and the right of men to treat their wives and children harshly and even kill them if they disobeyed, to the stories of a seven-day creation, a woman being formed out of man's rib, a virgin birth, and a flooding of the whole planet, are just a few of the biblical claims that must have bothered Descartes.

My point is that Descartes logically knew that we all believe things that we later find out are wrong, and he understood that he was in the middle of a social and cultural debate and so had to be very careful. Power was at stake. Getting in the middle of a fight between the Church and science was risky. Rather than being reckless, cowardly, or dogmatic, Descartes wrote systematically, thoughtfully, and modestly. He suggested waiting until a time when he could really think deeply and then, and only then, apply his mind, and ask what exactly is open to doubt. Actually even before looking into specific content he asks about form. He asks, and considers, what method he could apply to answer the question of what is open to doubt. Descartes understands that one cannot live life while radically doubting everything, for one must get along in the world; but he does understand the dialectics of doubt and is willing to explore the many sides of doubt. He does this by finding a form appropriate, not for living one's life, but for radical, philosophical analysis. His method, his form, only makes sense in context.

Utilizing a radical, and almost irrational, version of skepticism, Descartes knows he need not examine all his particular beliefs. He knows that would be an impossible task anyway. His method is such that he will treat as false anything he cannot prove true. The model here is deduction, and it draws heavily from mathematics. Still, it is a dialectical game in which he will only accept something as true if there is no rational or logical determinate negation to the claim. The determinate negation need not be plausible; it must only be possible within the realm of what is formally logical. An affirmative way of stating this is that Descartes will only accept something he can trust 100%. Further, the dialectical inquiry implies that, rather than examine all his particular beliefs, if he finds one example of a false belief he will reject the whole type of belief that it originated from or that it is associated with. He starts with the senses. The senses are the most obvious candidate for knowledge, since they seem to give immediate knowledge of the world. We open our eyes and we see the world, and seem to know it directly. As such, the senses are a strong candidate for building a foundation for knowledge. It seems obvious that we know the world through our senses. Thanks to our eyes, ears, tongue, skin, and nose we have sight, sound, taste, touch, and smell. But Descartes realizes right away that our senses sometimes deceive us. When we look in the distance, we sometimes think we see our friend, and as we move closer we realize it's not our friend, it's someone else. Of course things such as mirages also tell us we cannot 100% trust our senses.

But as a good interlocutor to himself, Descartes says that this is true for things far away but asks what about applying the senses to oneself? Surely, when Descartes looks at his own hand, it must be true that he is looking at his hand. He could never be deceived about that. Then he realizes that he is a vivid dreamer. At night sometimes his dreams are so vivid that he doesn't know he is dreaming. He starts to wonder if he is dreaming rather than writing the meditation at that moment. Could he be dreaming that he is looking at his hand, could he be dreaming that he is writing about looking at his hand? If he is dreaming, then he is not looking at his hand. If it is possible that he cannot distinguish his waking state from his dreaming state, and if there is no test to prove it either way, then he cannot even trust his senses when applied to his own body. His body, the house of the senses, the place of the eyes, ears, nose, tongue, and skin, may be an internal, deceptive house. In effect, he himself might be a haunted house. His body is perhaps a house of distorting mirrors, or a place filled with spirits, or a wonderland, a deceptive wonderland. Or, conceivably, he has no body.

15

If Descartes cannot trust the validity of the world or his body, since the senses that seem to validate them may be fallacious, then he must look into his mind and ask what he can be certain of regardless of whether he is awake or sleeping. He distinguishes between sciences that are *a priori* and those that are *a posteriori*. Things such as medicine, physics, and astronomy rely on the senses and so are *a posteriori*, while things like arithmetic and geometry do not rely on the senses and so are *a priori*. Descartes concludes that *a priori* things are the same regardless of whether he is awake or dreaming. Even while dreaming, he cannot contradict the laws of mathematics. Numbers work the same way as in the waking world; the laws of geometry hold even while dreaming. We don't dream of six-sided figures that are also perfect circles. For a moment, it seems, mathematics could be Descartes's foundation for knowledge. But Descartes is too dialectically astute to stop here. In his version of determinate negation he posits the mother of all counterexamples.

Descartes is careful to not implicate himself while suggesting that someone might assert that, rather than a perfectly good God existing, perhaps God is all-powerful, all-knowing, and naughty. It is logically possible that God is not perfectly good, in fact perhaps God is bad, and puts God-energy into deceiving Descartes. If so, then God could deceive Descartes not only concerning the world and the body, but also the mind itself. Everything within Descartes's mind could be false. The content of his mind could be full of false beliefs. Meditation One starts with Descartes acknowledging that he had false beliefs in his youth, and it ends with him wondering if everything in his mind, even at the present moment, is false. Meditation One, then, presents us with a radical critique of all knowledge through a Cartesian-style, hyperbolic method of doubt, that really is a version of determinate negation. Every claim he asserts he also negates with a specific counterexample, and he does so without replacing or transcending the negation, and yet the dialectic advances. Like the later Adorno, it remains a negative dialectic that shows the gaps and fissures between each object of inquiry and the concept trying to capture it. Descartes does not gloss over the gaps or fissures. He recognizes that the concept can never fully capture the object; it cannot even trust that the object is real, or that there is an object. And yet, the object, as thought through the mind, cannot be gotten rid of. There is no affirmation in this first mediation. Still, it lays the groundwork for Meditation Two. In this way one could say that the assertion that everything is false is an affirmation, and this is true only in the Hegelian sense of something being what it is precisely as it is becoming what it is not. If everything is false, everything could not be false, since the statement everything is false would be true. This point only validates the truth of dialectics.

Meditation Two starts with Descartes acknowledging that the game he is playing might be unwinnable. The game is to find one true thing, one thing that cannot be doubted. But this game of ultimate skepticism is tricky. When people start to question tradition or interrogate their beliefs, they might quickly find out that their tradition or beliefs are not so rationally justified. We believe some really silly and stupid things. Some of these things we even know are untrue, but still we cling to them. (One may know that not all Republicans are idiots, but nonetheless find it difficult not to believe that all Republicans are idiots. Seriously, how could anyone who is not an idiot support a party that would choose Sarah Palin for VP?)

Descartes experiences, at the beginning of Meditation Two, the feeling that people might get when they give up their political party but are not ready to join another party. If you are fed up with the Democrats, and you don't believe in them anymore, it doesn't necessarily mean that you will join the Republican Party. But not joining either party puts you in a state of nihilism. In a sense you believe in nothing, because not believing in either party puts you outside of politics. Some people will proudly claim to be independents, or non-voters. But this is silly. They either don't want to grow up and choose, or they are scared of embracing their nihilism. Either a Democrat or a Republican is going to win, and if you don't support either one then you are tantamount to a political nihilist; you are playing a game rather than dealing with reality.

Of course, the irony is that we could transcend the two-party system. If every one of us voted third-party, we could blow up our irrational system. In this sense, those who refuse to participate, or those who vote independent, are the admirable and demystified ones among us. Their lack of participation or third-party participation reveals a deeper truth about the system and our ability to change it. By accepting the two-party system, by participating in it, we make it seem natural and inevitable. Yet it is not natural or inevitable. Rather we are creating and recreating it through our actions. The system is not outside us; it is us. But we are alienated, in a Cartesian way, a type of mind/body dualism, a Democratic/Republican dualism. And these dualisms are false. There is no structural difference between the two parties. And just as "mind" tries to trick us into thinking it is separate from and more vital than body, the two-party system tries to trick us into thinking it is necessary, natural, and inevitable. Both mind and the two-party system are not independently real, not autonomous; they are not outside us. We reify ourselves and the political system when we forget that mind is just a word for our conscious, material selves, and when we forget that the system is our creation. The "system" is just people voting or not voting. It is democratic in that we could vote and elect a third-party candidate.

But at this point in history we don't trust ourselves. Likewise, at this point of the argument, Descartes does not trust himself. He feels as if he is drowning. He's treading water. But one can only tread water so long. At some point you have to swim to the other side or go back to shore. Treading water can be a good thing, and one can grow from it, get stronger from it, but at some point you have to choose, take a stand, and pick a side. According to Descartes, this means finding one true thing or admitting that there is no absolute truth. If it's the former, he can begin to build a house of knowledge on his foundational truth; and if it's the latter, he can go on living while accepting that everything is only contingent and merely probable.

17

If there is an evil genius, a *deus deceptor*, Descartes knows that the content of any of his beliefs might be false. But what about the form? Where does belief come from? Descartes concludes that it must come from the mind. Even to be deceived, he must exist; his mind must exist, for otherwise there would be nothing or no one to deceive. As he puts it: " 'I am, I exist' is necessarily true every time I utter it or conceive it in my mind."[1] There are many ways to articulate it: I think, therefore I am — Je pense, donc je suis — I am, therefore I exist — Cogito ergo sum. The point here is that thought, he thinks, needs a thinker. This I, this self, is a thinking thing, it is a mind, or perhaps even a soul. Bodies do not think. Or do they? Do brains? Do computers? Do cats? Descartes is forced to say they do not. Only minds think. But does thought even require a thinker? Descartes assumes it does. Is a mind material? Is it part of the brain? Descartes says it is not. Meditation Two is where we get a robust articulation of Cartesian dualism, mind/body dualism. We are two-fold beings: minds and bodies. As minds, our essence is thought. What is thought? It is affirming, denying, doubting, and even feeling. Yes, feeling. To perceive or feel heat is an activity of the mind. It seems like it should not be dependent on mind so much as body, yet Descartes is questioning that notion. We can perceive or feel heat, or think we do, even if we are dreaming.

This is exciting because it gives substance to the mind, or even better, the soul. If the soul can give us the substance of life without the body, then not only is there hope to survive the death of the body, but there is hope of a robust life after the body. If you can feel sexy without a body and someone else can look sexy without a body, well then heaven might be alright. And hell could be a hell of a time. But at this stage of the argument Descartes has only proved that he, as a thinking thing, exists, and as a thinking thing

1 Descartes, *Meditations on First Philosophy*, p. 18.

it means he can feel, sense, doubt, and so on. Still there is the problem of solipsism. Descartes knows he exists. He must exist if he can be deceived. But everyone else could be a figment of his imagination. Everyone else and everything else could be a construction of the *deus deceptor*.

Without knowing beyond a shadow of a doubt that the body exists Descartes still defines it by contrasting it with the essence and modes of the mind. The body's essence is extension. Bodies exist in space and time and have size, shape, location, and number. A self, a thinking self, in principle, can exist under the Cartesian logic without having a human body, or — any body — at all. One could be a brain in a vat, or stuck in the matrix, or a figment of someone else's dream, or a butterfly, or a computer virus, and so on. One can logically doubt that he has a body. To say "I doubt I have a body" seems unlikely, but it is logically possible to doubt. But if one says "I doubt I have a mind," she proves she has a mind. It takes a mind to doubt a mind.

18

Now Descartes's method requires that he not believe anything unless he is 100% certain. Is "I am, I exist" 100% certain every time one utters or thinks it? Perhaps. And perhaps not. It does assume that we can trust language, and logic; it assumes thinking needs a thinker. Do concepts need objects? Do objects need concepts? Do subjects need objects? Are subjects also objects? Can we trust language? Is logic infallible when it comes to the world? Can thinking exist without a thinker? Does consciousness require a self? The point here is that the dialectic is always already in place so that "I think therefore I am" is engulfed in a plethora of dialectical dualisms and assumptions from the first articulation.

We can see then in Meditation Two that Descartes is moving beyond theism and atheism, beyond subject/object dualism, whether he knows it or not. Descartes, in articulating Cartesian dualism, is undermining this dualism and showing the priority and necessity of an active, material subject, not just epistemologically but ontologically. For despite the claim that mind is the only sure thing his argument necessities thought, actions, others, and a world. These are all dialectically and internally connected to any articulation of "I think, therefore I am." Perhaps Descartes is unwittingly giving a proto-Marxist argument where mind is superstructure, body is state, and world is base. Reconfigured with these terms Cartesian dualism is overcome as we see ourselves in our bodies and in the world as much as in thought, as the articulation of thought is an action in the world. Mind, body, and world work together as base, state, and superstructure work together. There is no need to posit essentially distinct substances, no clean dualisms, just human actions feeding human ideas and theories, which in turn nourish or poison the body and the world.

19

In any case we have moved well beyond Descartes here. Descartes ends Meditation Two insisting that he only knows that he exists as a thinking thing. His body and the world cannot be proved and he uses his famous wax example to argue this. Imagine you see a bit of wax in a room. Imagine you are British (just because). You hold the wax and observe its white color, it makes a thud when you hit it on the floor, it smells like honey and flowers, it tastes like wax, it feels hard and smooth. Then imagine you put it by the fire and leave the room. When you come back into the room, you don't say "Oh my god! Who stole my bit of wax and replaced it with this lump of mush?" Rather, you say "My bloody wax melted." What interests Descartes is that your senses should be registering a different object. The color is no longer white, it makes no sound when you try to hit it on the floor; it smells like burnt wax, it tastes like chicken, and it feels soft and mushy. How do we know it's the same object? Descartes wants to credit the mind and innate ideas. Our minds not only prove we exist, but they are set up with ideas loaded into them. One naturally thinks that what philosophers call secondary ideas are partly mind dependent. Things such as taste, smell, touch and so on depend partly on us, not just the object. Thai food tastes as it tastes partly because of the food, and partly because of how our bodies and mind experience it. Thai food, to your dog, tastes differently, if it has any taste at all to a creature that just seems to inhale food. Descartes also, though, is claiming that primary qualities depend partly on us. Things like the size, shape, and location of an object needs a subject to grant or guarantee, or distinguish the object's existence. In the case of the wax, what it really proves is that we exist. If the wax is imaginary, if the evil genius is making us think it exists when it really doesn't, then we still know we exist in order to be deceived about it. And so long as we are thinking about it, then it exists, at least, in thought.

We can understand Descartes's reasoning here by applying it to the question, "If a tree falls in the woods and no one is around to hear it, does it make a sound?" The implication from Descartes is no. Sound is dependent on a receiver, someone or something to pick up the sound waves and convert them into sound. Sounds don't exist without hearers, and objects might not exist without subjects. Maybe the world is comparable to sound. Maybe even the world is a relational "object" than needs subjectivity to come into being. Maybe the smallest unit of reality is a relation, not a thing. Even the sound waves were created through interaction and relationships. Perhaps the universe itself is a dialectical one, an active, material, world of relations.

It may turn out that Bishop Berkeley was sort of, or partly, correct after all. "To be is to be perceived" claims Berkeley, but he doesn't go far enough. To perceive one needs to be a material thing. One needs an eye and a brain. To perceive is to be a materiality. Just as Marx had to turn Hegel right-side up, we might have to turn thinkers such as Descartes and Berkeley on their feet. We do have feet, more than we have souls. We see where we have to walk to make Descartes coherent, to solve the problems of philosophy. We need to leave philosophy and solve them in reality. We have to get to Marx. In Dante's *Inferno* he had to go through all the stages of hell to finally get to Satan and get out of and past hell. Satan was frozen, and upside down, and Dante had to walk over Satan to get out. We must do the same to get out of the God/atheism hellhole. We do this by going through Descartes's philosophy. And if Descartes's philosophy actually leads to the destruction of mind/body dualism, then maybe hell did just freeze over.

20

I am, I exist. Such is Descartes's one true thing. In Descartes's mind "I am, I exist" only proves he is a *thinking* thing. But this is not enough. Descartes wants to build a house of knowledge. But any belief, beyond knowing that as a thinking thing he exists, could be false because of the evil genius. How can Descartes get rid of the evil genius? What could defeat or refute a being that is all-powerful, all-knowing, and a naughty boy? In Meditation Three Descartes searches inside his mind to see what else is in there. There is much. There are ideas, volitions, and judgments. Some things seem to come from the outside world, some things seem to be inventions from Descartes himself, and some seem to be inside him but neither created by him nor by the outside world. In fact, one idea is essentially different — the idea of God. In his mind Descartes has the idea of God. What is this idea? It is the idea of a being that is omnipotent, omniscient, and omnibenevolent. God, as idea, is perfect. Now Descartes wonders how and where he got this idea. It does not seem to come from the outside world. The outside world is not perfect. Also, Descartes understands that he could not have thought up such a big idea. After all, little René may be quite good at math, exceptional even, yet the idea of God is essentially bigger and qualitatively different. Why couldn't Descartes think of God? Well, Descartes doubts, so Descartes knows he is not perfect. A being that is perfect would have no room for doubt. Yet he has the conception of perfection. Only a perfect being could create a perfect idea, and only a perfect being could put the idea of a perfect God inside of Descartes. After all, "What is more perfect cannot come into being from what is less perfect."[1] Descartes has the idea, the idea had to come from somewhere,

---

1 Descartes, *Meditations on First Philosophy*, p. 28.

it could only come from God — ergo God exists. Descartes discovers God in his head. Not only does God see all, but God is everywhere, even in your head. God is the ultimate peeping Tom.

Now that Descartes has proved God's existence, he can be sure that his worries about the evil genius were unfounded. For God, in all God's goodness, would never let another being systematically deceive Descartes. And in fact the evil genius cannot exist. If God is all-powerful then there cannot be another creature also all-powerful. It's logic, dear Watson! If something is all-powerful, there cannot be another equal to it. At most there could be a powerful, malicious creature — Satan — who can be quite wicked but cannot match God. Satan cannot defeat God and cannot even seriously challenge God, any more than you or I could.

21

As a kid I grew up on a beautiful lake in Michigan. A buddy and I used to go fishing and we would catch perch, and when lucky, bass and walleye, and when really lucky a pike. My parents had friends who had a nice property with a big house and a trout pond. The owner built the trout pond and stocked it himself. Sometimes my buddy and I would take a little boat from the lake to the river, dock the boat, and sneak onto my parent's friend's property and fish in their trout pond. We would catch a couple of trout and leave. One day, out of boredom, we threw some perch that we had caught from the river into the trout pond. One Sunday, at church, I heard the man telling my dad that he had perch in his trout pond. He knew some kids must have thrown them in. He built the pond, stocked it, and cared for it, and so he knew the other fish came from the outside. This is Descartes's reasoning. He looks into his own mind and finds an idea, that of a perfect God. It is inside his mind and yet he knows it didn't come from him or the world. It must have come from God, from the Big Fish.

With God "proved," Descartes can build his house of knowledge. If God exists there cannot be an evil genius, and without an evil genius Descartes gets his beloved mathematics back. The first brick for his house of knowledge is the *cogito*, the second is God. The only reason to doubt math, to doubt *a priori* truths, was when there was potentially an evil genius. With God as brick, there can be no evil genius, and so there is no reason to doubt mathematics. This is brilliant. The third brick is mathematics (arithmetic and geometry). Science now rests on God. God's perfection guarantees that the scientific principles of our world will be rational and good. God secures science; science rests on God. Science can study nature and the world; it can study anything that has extension. Yet science cannot speak to that which is unnatural, supernatural, or without extension. God is the buffer between science and the soul. Science cannot penetrate to the true self; it cannot touch the mind. The mind is defined by thinking, it is not measurable by science; it is actually the soul. Despite this conclusion Descartes transcends both God and atheism. Obviously he is not an atheist and yet he transcends religion as conceived at his time — he decenters God. Descartes's God is more akin to the God of deism; God just secures the world and the *cogito*. God set up a perfect world and does not need to intervene. Descartes's God does as much work today as if there were no God. Descartes only gestures to God.

22

A Cartesian-style philosophy must be careful, though, not to turn the cogito into a fetish. In the Kierkegaard essay of *Soul and Form*,[1] Lukács rejects the idea that form alone can fully redeem life. Life is more than form, and yet life cannot actualize without form. The Cartesian cogito needs life, needs content, as much as the world needs form to come into being. Together they redeem human life. Human form is internally linked to content. A thinking thing, without content, would not be a thing. It would not exist or be intelligible any more than Kant's thing-in-itself. The Cartesian starting point then is really a style, and only nominally a starting point, for there is no starting point, and the truth of the cogito must be cashed out through its own internal genre.

A theory, even a cool Cartesian one, does not capture life. Lukács understood that life is outside form, it is outside mind, although mind, as form, gives it expression. Form and mind don't exist without content and bodies. Each exists through the other although they can be analytically distinguished. Form isn't formed until it blends with content. And this is why form can fail. Lukács shows this through Kierkegaard's attempt to give form to life through a gesture. The gesture took the form of Kierkegaard breaking off his engagement to Regine Olsen; he withdrew from her. Despite the form, Kierkegaard failed to communicate his gesture so that Regine suffered and he carried guilt. His gesture didn't materialize. The point is that one doesn't need to infer dualism for a form or a mind to "fail." Action itself can fail since actions, by definition, are fallible. They are contingent practices. Materialism itself holds the possibility of failure, since other material, or Others, can push back on us. Dualism, understood as two essentially different substances, is not necessary to make sense of the world.

---

1 See *Soul and Form* chapter three.

The Cartesian gesture of "I am, I exist" fails in the same way as Kierkegaard's gesture failed since it did not materialize. Idealism, even just as a foundation, is dangerous. Descartes claimed that God told him not to get married, in a dream, and Kierkegaard also took wedding advice from the world's oldest bachelor. Kierkegaard's sacrifice of Regine was based on a mistaken mind/body dualism. Kierkegaard thought he had to sacrifice a personal life to complete himself, but this was because he had a fetishized view of the self and the world. His metaphysical approach convinced him he had to sacrifice the personal in order to be. While it is true that the cogito is personal, I only know that I exist, yet it does not follow that one must sacrifice everything else. Rather one should "sacrifice" the self. In the case of Kierkegaard, sacrificing himself rather than Regine would have saved both of them. In the case of the cogito, sacrificing the solipsism of the cogito, for the body, and through the body, for others, and through others, saves the cogito. It materializes it, demystifies it, and saves the truth of it. The cogito cannot function without the body despite the formalistic and abstract logic that it ought to. Kierkegaard couldn't function without Regine, although his metaphysical logic taught him he should.

What Kierkegaard thought of as a limit was actually the condition of possibility to form himself completely. The gesture of breaking off an engagement was the wrong limit, a misinterpreted limit. Kierkegaard misunderstood the dialectical truth of his gesture. He thought his gesture was personal. It was. Yet it also dialectically became a political and social act. A Cartesian limit need not make this mistake. Descartes's philosophy shows the task of forming oneself gets underway once a limitation is set, a withdrawal from idealism and immature materialism, is what actually motivates the process of form-making. Descartes's gesture, his articulation of his existence, was personal, and at the same time it was a political and social act. Descartes's *Meditations* did protect science from the irrationalities of the Church and it did help usher in modernity. It had the practical effect of dissolving the conflict between science and religion. As philosophy, as superstructure the proof of the mind is ideological. It came from the base as it shook the base.

Descartes gesture of "I am, I exist," as typically interpreted, stays trapped in traditional Cartesian dualism, in the world's dualism. His gesture is viewed as an instrumental act to prove his existence. Yet it is actually intrinsically meaningful and points the way to who Descartes is, and to who we are, not just *that* he is or *that* we are. In this way Descartes's cogito really is a solid foundation, but without being foundational. It is simply the coming together of form and content through an act, a gesture. And it exists when it comes together. Like a joke. The *Meditations* is a joke. All comics know that witty people hear their joke when they say their joke. They don't first think it and then say it. In these moments form, content, and life are one. Within the act, the gesture, the totality is captured.

None of this is to say it's completely internal, though. Language, especially the "I am, I exist" aims to understand and communicate; but this understanding and communicating cannot happen without some sort of externalization (and in fact comes from externalization, from history). The successful gesture, like successful wit, is a gesture toward truth and in the name of truth. Descartes could only gesture, could only write the *Meditations*; anything more would have gotten him locked up or killed. Sometimes anything more than a gesture will kill truth and understanding. Sometimes a gesture, a joke, is the truest thing.

Chapter 4. Marx On the Trolley

1

Certainly a long time has passed since Francis Fukuyama famously predicted that we have reached the end of history, and yet despite the absurdity of the thesis, the status quo remains. Initially it provided good fodder for conferences, seminars, debates, and other carnivalesque activities. Today, though, it takes on a different significance. Ultimately, if we cannot transcend into something beyond the present, then our given world, full of wars, religious extremism, rapid climate change, and an unprecedented consumption of the earth's finite resources will literally cause the end of human history.

Our stage of history, which supposedly rests on capitalism and democracy, heavily tilts toward the capitalist side. The world is being run by the Capitalist-Kings who have abandoned their Straussian sidekicks. Still these associates, no different than Kalinin in Kundera's novel *The Festival of Insignificance*, hope to have a city named after themselves. And they do deserve it for the role they played in destabilizing the Middle East. We shall name their city Straussgrad. The Straussgrad festival will endlessly celebrate itself, like a fox on the news, under the spell of an eclipse, where even the caves within the cave need esoteric names.

Yet in the Straussgrad cave one might notice that the blood moon penetrates deeply into the clay and makes all the balloons different shades of rouge as history foreshadows itself. But to give up the balloons requires letting go of power and fear, letting go of the balloons being held so tightly with those pudgy white fingers, and it requires exiting the cave (and perhaps blowing it up); otherwise the balloons simply rise a few feet into the air and then hit against the cavern roof. We have all seen the look of frustration on a child's face when she loses hold of a balloon and it hovers so gently above, tapping along the ceiling. No, it's better when the balloon is released into the open air with no chance of recovery. One must accept the balloon is gone and learn to live without it. No ladder, not even Wittgenstein's, can retrieve it. Mythic fear, which grows in deluded academic soil, is much harder to let go of than ancient mythos. The latter can be transcended by better stories while the former thinks it is grounded in esoteric truth and a higher morality, bequeathed to them by a lion named Leo. But some prophets really just are old astrological names.

Fukuyama, however, should be commended for showing a learning curve, but instead he paid the price of exile. His accusers though, in an apish mimesis of Aristophanes' soulmates and Darwinian selection, deduced that half chimps–half bonobos could transcend into Übermenschen with only the occasional lapse into sex and violence. These digressions supposedly would be rendered innocuous through an appeal to different moralities for different (read "higher") types. Rationalization triumphs. While elite and herd morality sounds plausible to these ears, any mention of communism gets shouted down as romantic or weak. A man cannot maintain the whole misguided self-image of the lucky few without shunning the C-word. Today, many are still walking around with copies of Machiavelli's *The Prince* prominently tucked under their pasty rail-like arms. Unknowing gnomes.

2

Like Fukuyama's thesis, the Trolley Problems[1] have been around for a while. These are moral puzzles that ask us to give our intuitions when it comes to situations in which we have to choose whom we save and whom we don't, in life and death situations. Undergraduates especially enjoy these, and it is good entry into moral philosophy. These amusing yet seemingly unrealistic puzzles have actually shown use value as they have entered into the conversation with engineers who are tasked with programming self-driving cars. If a self-driving car is going to hit someone who happens to be in the road and there is no time to stop, when should the car continue forward and when should it swerve? What is the appropriate ethical program to put into the machine when the choice is between running over pedestrians vs. crashing the car into a wall, potentially killing the driver and passengers? Turns out the trolley problems might have more direct real life application than they are usually given credit for. In any case, one thing the trolley

---

1 I learned the Trolley Problems from the philosopher John Martin Fischer but he is in no way responsible for my interpretation of them. Fischer's teachings and writings on the Trolley Problems offers a model for how to do exquisite analytic philosophy. This chapter is nothing like that.

problems bring out rather quickly is the importance of utilitarian thinking, and almost as quickly they show the limits of this thinking. Let's briefly look at the three most basic cases.

In scenario one, there is a trolley rolling out of control and it is going to crash into an innocent person at the end of the tracks. You are positioned farther up the track, and it so happens that you can pull a lever that will shoot the trolley onto another track, and in so doing save the innocent life. That sounds good, right? But then you realize that on this other track five innocent people are trapped and will be killed if you pull the lever. (That will teach you for hanging out around trolley tracks.) Still, it is clear to delinquents, and to pretty much everyone, that you should not pull the lever; you unfortunately have to do nothing. But if you happen to be a Hegelian, you can at least enjoy knowing that doing nothing is really doing something. Still, one must feel for the innocent trapped in an analytic moral puzzle. The point, though, is that it would be wrong to pull the lever. Unfortunately you have to let the one person die rather than intervene, for that would kill five. Of course if you know the one person, your intuition and your choice might change. But that's not the point, and that's another puzzle. The point here is to attempt to determine what the morally correct response is when forced to decide between two unhappy choices, and where everyone involved is innocent and of equal worth to you. These puzzles assume a modern sensibility, one in which everyone is *a priori* presumed equal. Case one also hints that even if one has a tribal mentality, even when we care more about "our" people, we all pretty much know that we are violating a moral intuition if we choose our one over the many others. Killing five to save one person you care about may be the choice you make, but I doubt you will try to claim it is the moral choice.

Getting back to the original situation then, what does this first scenario teach us? It seems that morality and maximizing human life are connected. Perhaps, philosophically, the interesting thing is that we see that morality is largely about trying to do the most good or avoid the most pain. We don't have to get all mystical or metaphysical, or even bring God into it. Rather, maximizing human happiness and minimizing human pain seems to be a good thing almost universally. Of course, it is much more complicated than that. One could ask about motives, and duties to other things including animals and nature, or obligations to one's group, and so on. Interesting questions, but none of this is really going to talk us out of thinking that if you can save more human beings, everything else being equal, it's probably a good thing.

3

The second standard trolley case is to reverse the positions of the innocents — now five will die if you don't pull the lever. The trolley is on a track leading to five people's death. You could pull a lever and divert the trolley, but now you will be directly responsible for the trolley switching tracks and killing one. If morality is only about the numbers, then everything else being equal, it seems you should pull the lever and save the five. Still, it would be hard to do, and it makes some people question whether it is the right thing. Should we be "playing God"? Should one actively intervene to save people when other (although fewer) individuals will die as a result? It's not a happy situation. Military decisions often involve calculations of this sort, so you can imagine the stress and anxiety for those unfortunate enough to have to attempt to calculate odds. This is especially difficult in real life, for we never have certainty, as the consequences of our actions are often unpredictable. In real life, sometimes, what seems to be the wise choice, the choice that will save more people, turns out to be wrong.

4

The third case, The Fat Man Case, besides not being PC, requires a seemingly more direct action. The trolley is out of control again, but this time your only chance of stopping it, since now there is no second track, is to push a very large gentleman onto the track. His sheer bulk will stop the trolley and save the five others from being crushed, but he will surely die. What do you do? Do you push him? Should you push him? Is morality only about the numbers, or is there more going on?

The trolley problems are useful devices for thinking about morality, but what use can they be in a discussion of Marxism? Marx himself would probably have little patience for them, but a Marxist could argue that since these cases appear in our classrooms, in books, and in our lifeworld, and since philosophy is part of the superstructure, these cases should tell us something about the inner workings of our society. Why is it that these cases speak to us, why do they interest, excite, and motivate students to study philosophy? Perhaps they mirror, rationalize, and distort our actual world. Maybe they signal that we are living in a world that values abstract, unrealistic, mathematical, quantification-like reasoning and that is why we find them so appealing. Maybe they help rationalize how we actually think today. And they even might be relevant for showing us the contradictions of our capitalist society. We live in a world where we are constantly sacrificing others or ourselves. At this point in history it is rather pathetic that so many still get sacrificed, and so often we get put in morally ambiguous situations.

Obviously life and death are not so directly at stake in most of our day-to-day lives, but if we look under the surface of our world just a little, we will see that we are implicitly making trolley-type decisions every day; but we are not acknowledging it or attempting to philosophically come to terms with these choices. At best we sometimes have abstract debates about them, but the contradictions between our beliefs and our actions never get resolved. We just keep doing the same things. We keep buying Nike shoes, using plastic bags, purchasing gas guzzling cars, consuming factory-farmed meat, sending young men and women into wars of choice, and we could go on and on. If Marxist philosophy is going to speak through the trolley problems, it will have to bring in history and society. But first we will begin by moving thin to thick.

The trolley problems make salient the difference between utilitarian reasoning and deontological ethical theory. They highlight the advantages and disadvantages of both. When looking at things instrumentally, when considering utility, one just compares the numbers. When you can save five rather than one, it's an instrumental success and so it is ethical. Yet when you get to the fat man example, utilitarian thinking becomes problematic. It seems obviously wrong to directly use a human being in order to save some others down the track. The trolley problems get us thinking about the conflict between trying to save as many people as possible and trying not to use people in the process. The trolley problems show how quickly this can become a conflict. Figuring out which one to give preference to in each situation is part of the art of acting ethically. But what happens when you are in a situation where any action is both instrumentally and intrinsically problematic? Here, don't we need to change the whole puzzle?

In capitalist society both the intrinsic good and the instrumental good get thwarted. Most people don't thrive in a capitalist society. Capitalist society favors the few, the minority at the top. Most people are exploited in our system of wage labor. Our resources are being gobbled up, our environment is becoming more polluted, our climate is warming, and future generation's needs and interests are not even visible on our track. Also, intrinsically, most people do not enjoy their jobs; they feel alienation from their work, others, and even from themselves in the workplace and in society at large. People try to distract themselves just to get through the day. They bury their heads in their cell phones as they try to escape from their situation. This phenomenon spills over into the rest of our modern world as most of our lives are not focused on the intrinsic, the present, or the internal; most of the time we are living for the weekends, so to speak. And when the weekend comes, we find out it's not what we thought it was going to be. The party was lame, the game a bore, the meal too expense. Most of our best moments and memorable weekends will be anti-capitalist, and yet the mantra of capitalism is America's religion. America rides the trolley track of capitalism and anyone who questions it is labeled a traitor. Still, it' worth repeating: the best times are when we are off the capitalist track, when we are engaged in non-commodified activities, and when we are with those we care about and love. Yet our society is built upon separating us. You have to take the job where there is the job, and take your vacation week when the company decides, and so on. No need to say more, because those of us who work real jobs, which is to say most of us, understand.

Against the irrational and immoral system that supposedly makes our country great, we understand what's important. When our being-in-the-world is soaking up tranquil nature, or vibrant city, or when we are with our pets or children at the park, or doing service to others, or hanging out with others within civil society, these moments are intrinsically worthwhile and will hold in our memories. These sorts of activities need not involve stupid consumption and are even better if no pictures (and especially no selfies) are taken, no tweets sent out, and no showboating takes center stage. It's just you and those you care about, together, in such a way that nothing else matters at that moment.

These times also provide contrast to a bad sort of instrumentality. What results from these intrinsically motivated activities is a better future life, an ability to experience and share in more robust human activities, as these times indirectly lead to a better future. Contrast this with the rest of one's life in which one feels used and abused, trapped in unfortunate trolley-like situations. After all, the normal mode of operation today is one where most people are being pushed around no less than the fat man, and so don't feel phat. Most people get used daily, and most of the time we are not maximizing the good. The one percent gets saved and the rest suffer. Further adding to the alienation and exploitation is the sense that we are living in the end of history. Utopian ideas are dead. How did we end up here? The history of Western philosophy offers a clue.

5

In Western philosophy, the idea of human nature develops out of the philosophy of Thales. Thales is considered the first philosopher, as he represents the idea that humans can discover truth without appealing to the supernatural. His focus was on *logos*, not *mythos*, as he pushed beyond the understanding of the poets. He is commendable in his ability to think outside the gods, yet he was not able to transcend a metaphysical foundation. One third solid, his metaphysical urge was quenched by insisting everything is water. His foundational approach set the terms and limits of the meaning of philosophy for a long time. With the emphasis on empirical reality and logical deduction the world became something intelligible through the use of cognition, and it became something that could be predicted and controlled thanks to reason. Socrates accepted his preference for *logos* over *mythos*, but directed his ambitions into the human and away from the natural world. The real Socrates would never fall into a well, but he might go on asking how well we know ourselves until someone throws him in. He would probably get pushed onto the trolley tracks. In this way Socrates combined theory and practice. Dying for one's beliefs, especially non-dogmatic beliefs, takes a special kind of courage. But what interests us is how Socrates connected abstract ideas such as courage to the practices of individuals and society. Would Socrates push the fat man?

The answer is suggested in how he responds to the challenge of the ring of Gyges. A couple of sophists, Straussian types, are recruiting a couple of youths into their club. They are offering, for a price I'm sure, to teach these youths the secret of living. The secret is that morality is a sham. Moral codes and legal principles are for suckers. The key to living well, though, is to keep this private, for the masses buy into the naïve ideas of gods, the good, and the right, and other useless trifles. The sophists in this dialogue propose that you can and should do whatever you please without guilt or conscience; you should take what you can in life, for you only go around once, as the saying goes. But you have to be a sneak. You have to maintain the perception of goodness, keep a clean reputation, so that the masses do not catch on and attempt to emulate you and so that the masses cannot punish you. They cement their pop psychology using the myth of the ring of Gyges.

One version of the myth goes like this. Gyges was your average Joe, not a sinner or a saint. He lived in his village following and living by the norms of his tribe. One day, while taking a walk in the woods, he comes across a ring resting in a broken tree. He puts on the ring and goes back to his village without really thinking about it. Hanging out, he fidgets with the ring on his finger and turns it. He realizes that his friends are talking about him as if he is not there. He realizes he is invisible. As his "nature" has changed, or now that he can acknowledge his true nature, Gyges recognizes that he would prefer to live differently. He realizes that he need not be constrained by the moral and legal norms he has always lived by. He realizes that he has only been moral and fair because he was worried about his reputation and he feared punishment from the law. Without these social constraints to hold him back, Gyges pounces. He waits until the drawbridge on the castle goes down, makes himself invisible, and crosses into the castle; he kills the King and takes the Queen. He takes over the Kingdom.

The Sophists claim we all would and should do that, if we had the power. And many with power actually do that. This is how the 1% lives. If the masses knew how the 1% really lives, they wouldn't believe it. If average people understood what bigwigs on Wall Street really do, and what they think of normal, hardworking Americans, they would be destroyed. The top percent in this country do think of the general public as "the masses," as weak and as fools. They think religious people are morons. They are amazed how the ignorant masses watch Fox news and vote against their own interests. They feel the masses deserve their fate because they are so stupid. The masses are so deluded by their religion, their patriotism, and their naïve beliefs that they convince themselves that perhaps one day they, or their children, will be on top. I'm sure Joe the Plumber still believes he's going to be somebody one day, yet to the elite he will always be a cretin fool. In this sense the elites enjoy a greater invisibility than Gyges with his magic ring. This is the gist of the conversation in *The Republic*: The Sophists are telling the elite youth how they can live like Gyges and why they ought to.

One might respond by pointing out that the ring of Gyges is just a myth and that if ordinary individuals are not respected by the elites, it doesn't really bother the average folk. They live their lives according to their own sense of morality and reason, and that's just fine. One might even add that most people do not have anything like the powers that an invisible ring grants to Gyges, so it's really a non-issue. Against this a social and historical approach insists that there is more at stake than simply dismissing the lesson of Gyges's Ring. What if the attitude and practices of the economic elites has saturated our lifeworld and structured how everyone acts and thinks. What if what Wall Street does actually matters? What if the economy is really the base?

6

Max Horkheimer argues for these points in *Eclipse of Reason*. He worries that the reasoning process of Gyges has become accepted and normalized in the modern world and yet we don't see it. In fact, according to Horkheimer, what passes for rationality today directly distorts modernity's potential and internally corrupts us as individuals. As he puts it, his book aims "to inquire into the concept of rationality that underlies our contemporary industrial culture, in order to discover whether this concept does not contain defects that vitiate it essentially."[1] He continues with the "reflections set forth in the book seek to relate the current *impasse* in philosophical thinking to the concrete dilemma of the human outlook for the future."

---

1 All my quotations in this section from Horkheimer are from his *Eclipse of Reason*, pp. v–1.

Horkheimer asks why is it that "even as technical knowledge expands the horizon of man's thought and activity, his autonomy as an individual, his ability to resist the growing apparatus of mass manipulation, his power of imagination, his independent judgment appear to be reduced. Advance in technical facilities for enlightenment is accompanied by a process of dehumanization. Thus progress threatens to nullify the very goal it is supposed to realize — the idea of man." In the Ancient Greek world, ordinary men voted Socrates to death, and in the modern one ordinary citizens helped vote Mussolini and Hitler into office.

In Christopher R. Browning's book *Ordinary Men*, he details how seemingly ordinary men, men who did not detest Jewish people, could so easily torture and kill them during the Hitler period. The simple pressure to conform to the group, to not look like a coward, was motivation enough for these ordinary men, not only willing to commit evil, but actually make it routine and even fun. Adding to this craziness is that after the war they went back to their regular lives, largely without guilt or reflection. Horkheimer, comparable to Socrates before him, sees our world as full of these "ordinary men." He says if you ask the ordinary man to define reason he will say that "reasonable things are things that are obviously useful, and that every reasonable man is supposed to be able to decide what is useful to him." In other words what makes reasonable actions possible is the "faculty of classification, inference, and deduction, no matter what the specific content — the abstract functioning of the thinking mechanism." Horkheimer calls this subjective reason and he sees it as connected intimately to the modern ability, not only to allow the holocaust, but to participate in it. Subjective reason goes no deeper than trying to solve problems given one's situation. What are the means one can use to satisfy the ends? The ends don't get challenged, or they get rationalized away, in the same way conservatives rationalize away the futility of dealing with climate change or gun control. They either deny the truth (the correlation between guns and killing, and the evidence that humans have caused climate change) or say "that's just how the world is." These denials and rationalizations keep the ends from being challenged in any serious way. Rather than using reason to understand the world and contemplate it, the ordinary man uses reason as a strategic tool to satisfy his subjective urges. And as soon as individuals accept the ends which are convenient for them, then they can rationalize the means. If the ends cannot be challenged then it would be illogical not to accept the means to those ends. It's the attitude promoted by a capitalist system, a system that encourages private vices and self-interest; it is the modern way of being-in-the-world, the ordinary way. As Horkheimer puts it, "It is essentially concerned with means and ends, with the adequacy of procedures for purposes more or less taken for granted and supposedly self-explanatory. It attaches little importance to the question whether the purposes as such are reasonable." The result is that, for the ordinary person, what counts as reasonable is what serves the narrow interests of the subject or the subject's tribal community. The nation kills Jews, the individual kills Jews. Subjective reason is merely the tool that helps one achieve success. Rather than analyzing the role reason plays, the ordinary man rationalizes in this manner: "Reason doesn't kill, people do. Horkheimer quit trying to take our subjective reason away." Horkheimer, like Socrates, understood the dangers of formalistic beliefs; empty dogmas that miss the connection between theory and practice. Subjective rationality, in a world sinisterly fed by a capitalist economy, is as dangerous as the 2nd Amendment, in a world sinisterly fueled by the NRA.

7

Just as today it is futile to try to convince extreme gun advocates of the irrationality of their position, Socrates does not directly take on the Sophist's rationalization of Gyges's actions. Just as guns give certain individuals a false yet seductive feeling of power and control, the Sophists gave their young listeners a seductive argument to feel powerful and in control. Socrates, knowing he cannot directly refute this argument, takes his interlocutors on an excursus, a trip, not to a mythical ancient village with magic rings but to a more realistic thought experiment examining what it would mean to found, or build, a city. Sophists, capitalists, and the NRA don't want to change society or make it better. It is in their narrow interests for the world to continue to run on fear and deception. Socrates, on the other hand, thinks beyond subjective reason and is willing to contemplate larger and better ways of living. He wants to show the young men how to become critical thinkers, how to become founders of a new city; and in so doing he shows them how to become dialectical philosophers.

Socrates says "the city is the soul writ large."[1] Before he will discuss why one should not use Gyges as a model for living, Socrates says it will be useful to talk about the construction of a city, an ideal city. The conversation leads to an agreement that the ideal city will consist of three parts — three different sorts of people all doing their bit are necessary for the city to function well. The highest part is the rulers. The rulers will govern the city and make the laws. They agree that the virtue most needed in a ruler is wisdom. The wise ruler will understand the relationship between theory and practice, and will be able to make decisions and laws that will allow for the city to thrive, to be successful. The second highest group is the guardians. Guardians are the warrior class, and they need the virtue of courage. Guardians must protect

1 See Plato, *The Republic*, Book II.

the city from internal and external threats, and they must also have the courage to enforce the rules and laws of the rulers. The final type consists of the craftsmen. Craftsmen and workers must materially reproduce the city. They must make sure that the city has enough food, shelter, clothing, goods, and artifacts. Socrates, somewhat surprisingly, says their most important virtue is moderation. One might think he would say their virtue should be skill at their craft. The fact that this is a nonissue for Socrates shows how skilled the Greeks were. Yet Socrates was concerned with overconsumption. Today that's an issue because we have so much, at Socrates's time it was an issue because of scarcity. They must not over consume or expect too much. They must respect the rulers and let them rule. They should not be too greedy, and must not let their baser instincts govern them. This is difficult but the rulers and guardians exist to help ensure maturity.

But what does this have to do with Gyges's ring? It is only after discussing the city that Socrates is positioned to make his point concerning individual virtue. Remember, the city is like "the soul writ large," meaning the individual is comparable to a city, and as such can be understood as having three essential parts, that when working together make one ideal. The individual should be ruled by reason. Our minds, with their ability to think, reflect, anticipate, look at the big picture, consider consequences and so on, are the key to living a meaningful, excellent, and successful life. Still, knowing what to do is not enough. One must have motivation and courage to do the right thing. We often know what to do, what is best for us, but we cannot muster the courage or energy to do it. This is where heart comes in. Socrates called this our spirited part. We might call it our will. But whatever you call it, you want it to side with your rational part so that your actions are driven by your wisdom. The final part of our three-fold nature Socrates calls the appetitive part. Freud called it the Id. This is the home of our passions and especially our sexual and violent energy. Socrates was not a prude. He did not think this energy was inherently bad, but in excess it is very destructive for human beings. We must keep our passions moderate if we want to live a free and happy life. If we want to be in control and mature we must let our reason rule us and bring out our appetitive part when it is acceptable to do so. Keeping these parts in harmony creates a state of health. This structure is intrinsically good because it is peaceful, advocates consciousness and self-awareness, and feels right. It is just nice to be doing the rational thing, to be in control, to let the passions out when it's the right time, and to feel that you have the courage to defend and create your best self. When wise beliefs are put into practice, and validated by reality, it is inherently satisfying. And, of course, it is instrumentally good. It keeps you from getting into trouble, you have more success and wins in life, and it leads to other goods. Living this life of internal harmony and external consistency makes one proud and makes those who matter proud also.

Now we can consider Gyges again. When Gyges sneaks into the castle he is driven by his appetites and his lust. He is not doing the wise or ethical thing; rather he is just seizing power because he can. He has no care for what he is doing to himself on the inside or the outside. He has no care for what he is doing to his community, either. Killing the King and raping the Queen will not make him or those who care about him proud. Just as today, carrying a gun makes no one proud. The appetites drive fear and obsession over gun rights, not human reason. Those who think guns make them safer don't understand probability and are either ideologically deluded or just frightened and out of control, projecting their violence impulses onto the rest of the world. Socrates would not use Gyges's ring to become king; he would not need a gun; and he certainly would not push the fat man. Socrates will not act in an unwise or unethical manner. But Socrates also understands that individuality only exists in society, so he might be willing to pull a lever if it benefited the whole, even as it sacrificed one, or even five. One must know the role to play in the city, in the society, and have the courage to do the wise thing, which is also the ethical thing, and not be driven by irrational passion or fear. We have made the right choices in the trolley problems when we maintain our virtue and character, and the society's too. Our society and individuality must be protected, but not at the expense of losing our identity, or our virtue.

8

We see that Socrates had a robust understanding of the dialectical connection between the individual and society. The Middle Ages tried to reconcile both with heaven, and in so doing had to attempt to purge the human of the appetitive drives to ensure that the idea that the next world would remain pristine which, in turn, created an abyss between the actual world, with its brutality and corruption, and the holy world. This ideology exacerbated regressive dualistic thinking for both individuals and society, as it legitimated an unjust world and rationalized lack of trying to change it. Christian dualism forces one to accept the contradictory thesis of a pristine soul and corrupt body co-habiting a self. This leads to the desire to give up one of the two halves. Christian ideology assumes we will opt for the good, but it's more complicated than that. As long as we have bodies it's rather tricky to discard the flesh, so the other half is as likely to fall to the wayside. But realism, grounded in a dirty, bad self, doesn't always prompt history to travel to nicer destinations; Thomas Hobbes becomes a Christian foil and attempts, like Pavel Ivanovich Chichikov from Gogol's *Dead Souls*, to cash in.

Hobbes's brilliant idea was to abandon the idea of a better self hiding inside the outer animal and abandon the idea of a better world above. He opted for what he saw — an uncontrollable, brutal beast running deep throughout the human, and a cold, heartless world ever ready to plunge us into an even deeper abyss. We have never completely escaped this Hobbesian intuition. It brings us back to Fukuyama and suggests that the medieval world literally was the Middle Ages. That would make today nearing end times, which adds a perverted twist to the end-of-history thesis that we started this chapter with. According to Hobbes it doesn't matter what you choose in the trolley problems, because *you* are not choosing. You are just a program doing whatever the program was set to do. With Hobbesian red-eyes, there is no point in wasting our time wracking our brains about it; we should just let it go. We will all die soon enough anyway, so protect yourself, push them all, and let God or Gogol sort them out.

The bigger point though is that since Thales the dominant narrative has stuck to a quasi-deterministic vision of the self to be discovered by *logos*, and perhaps indirectly verified by *mythos*. In this Socrates and Hobbes are on the same page. Socrates is more sophisticated since he aims to discover an inner and outer, while with Hobbes that distinction doesn't exist. Still, both agree with Thales that there is a truth to be discovered, and once discovered, like other laws of nature, the self could be predicted and controlled, and taught to obey. The only question becomes whether we are naughty-Hobbesian, blank-Lockeian, or gentle-Rousseauian. Do we need more prisons, better government, or Montessori schools? These metaphysical notions, although in many ways unlike the ancient and medieval ontologies, nonetheless are still a kind of traditional metaphysics. We had to wait until Kant for this model to get really shaken up.

9

Unlike the major players before him, Kant's epistemology emphasizes activity and the subject's role in the construction of knowledge. As subjects we are endowed with stable categories that filter, structure, and organize a buzzing, blooming world out there. According to Kant these categories are not subject to history, culture, or the social. Outside the construction, Kant still holds to a traditional conception of metaphysics with his notion of "noumena" and his aversion to history. There is a world "out there" that transcends the human, but we have no access to it since our experience is a mediation of what's out there and what's in us. This thing-in-itself — *das Ding an sich* — is objective reality outside us; we cannot know it, but it is there. By positing a world out there, objects out there, Kant tempts the adventurous types into looking for a route to "out there." Perhaps one can bypass the mediation and directly experience the world as it is, truly, and that way directly, without mediation, come to find out what is really going on. Perhaps through meditation, drugs, prayer, deep cognition, exercise, sex, yoga, chanting, baroque music, Pink Floyd, Headspace, or whatever, one can make it to the other side unmediated. Perhaps not, says Hegel.

Hegel radicalizes Kant by rejecting the idea of noumena, and so he rejects a traditional conception of an objective world outside us, of objects that exist outside human experience. Hegel, as the philosopher of history, looks at the world in context and as process, and gives an account of how a historical subject processes the buzzing, blooming world. In a sense this world, as Hegelian conceived it, is crazier than the Kantian vision, for it is a world that is always moving, shifting, perhaps progressing. It is a world of conflict and opposites that are really not opposites. Further, for Hegel, it is not enough to look at individuals in isolation. We must look at the social, historical, and cultural, not simply the ahistorical and individual. Knowledge is subject to history, and individuality is predicated on the social. The famous example of someone trying to be a Samurai warrior today makes the point. No matter how badly one might want to be a Samurai warrior — perhaps one wants to study it in college, even major in it — nonetheless one cannot become one (although I'm sure some private online college will let you, if you ask nicely and pay their ridiculous tuition. One can imagine a Samurai Warrior major rising up like the phoenix from University of Phoenix). And it's not your fault. The world has moved on. So what it means to be a Samurai warrior cannot be fully understood by the modern mind nor actualized by the modern body. Modern society doesn't have the structure for it. We cannot convince ourselves of the social hierarchy that makes one willing to pull out his short blade and kill himself pre-reflectively, "naturally," if he has brought shame to himself. The world sets the conditions and limits for who and what we become. We can push those limits or pull back on them but we cannot completely transcend them.

Michael Jordan could only become the greatest basketball player in history (if he is) if there is a world that has basketball in it, if that world allows African Americans to play in the league, if Jordan has the right upbringing, teammates, luck, and so on. All this background provides the conditions for Jordan to emerge. He takes it from there. His insane competitiveness, incredible work ethic, intelligence, and focus are mediated through his moment of history and created his supreme excellence. The dialectic between Jordan the individual and American society is the necessary condition for Jordan, as the Jordan we know, to exist. Yet it's not a symmetrical dialectic. The priority goes to the social. The human world exists before Jordan, it conditions him, only then does he affect it, and his moment is fleeting, the basketball world predates him and continues even when the mighty Jordan is gone. We can explore this more deeply by constructing a free interpretation of Hegel's master–slave dialectic.

10

Hegel's master–slave dialectic views the development of consciousness as a movement toward freedom. We cannot be sure of our existence, our human existence, without recognition from others. Ideally we should recognize each other mutually, but mutual recognition is unlikely for beings with weak egos. We will attempt to prove our existence through force, with each willing to wager life to prove existence to the other. The threat of death is the only thing that will give each the recognition craved. Yet if one dies, there will be no acknowledgment so ultimately one, probably the smarter one, the more reflective one, gives in.

At this point one becomes the master and the other the slave; the one who doesn't give in or doesn't back down, makes the other the slave. Since the master spared the life of the slave, the slave gives the master the recognition craved. But the slave does not get recognition from the master. The master gets self-consciousness while the slave only receives semi-consciousness. The master gets recognition and forces the slave to do the labor. The master gets all needs met, and yet, this turns into a dialectical dead end.

The master becomes dependent on the slave. The master cannot make or do anything worthwhile; the master just desires and consumes. Meanwhile the slave gains self-consciousness through labor. The slave transforms nature and produces and externalizes and so creates a self, based on labor and interaction with the world. By interacting concretely with the world, the slave's self grows on the inside and is reflected in the world. The world reflects the slave's labor so that subject/object dualism begins to dissolve. The slave is transformed by the object of labor and the object of labor takes in the slave's effort. The self of the slave is in the object of labor as the object of labor is in the one who worked on it. In this way the slave is more than a slave. The slave is now a self, a self full of the world as the world is full of the transformed self. When the slave recognizes this, the slave is free. Knowledge then is first and foremost an action. We must act, we must put ourselves in the world before the world can reflect us. It is a process of creation so that the rigid ontological and epistemological dualism dissolves. The one who labors with reflective action comes to know the world as one creates the world. You come to know the self as you create the self. You come to know the self of your creation, and to know that this is the true self, and the world you are working on, is the true reality, the true world. The world and the self are only real and true through interaction, and action. The Hegelian secret then to knowing oneself is to thoughtfully create oneself while creating the world as a mirror of oneself.

If knowledge is a reflective action, then the final step is to recognize that one does not need the master and to act in such a way that one is no longer a slave. Hegel didn't make this last move but he did point out the irony through the dialectic. The most obvious irony is that the master is really the slave and doesn't know it. Further, both the master and the slave are seeking recognition from each other, but recognition will mean nothing unless there is equality and mutual respect. And further, this equality and mutual respect will mean nothing unless they are both actively engaged in the world. Two equal slave owners who respect each other do not move the dialectic forward. Still the dialectic outwits the original two in the struggle, for in reality the master is the slave and the slave the master, regardless of their subjective thoughts on the matter. In reality, which is to say in practice, the slave is the one acting, and becoming more and more educated concerning the social world and nature. Even before the slave realizes it, perhaps, the so-called slave has a strong ego because the slave is strong enough to survive, to work, and to overcome. The slave is strong and knowledgeable through action. More strength and more knowledge comes with deeper reflection, deeper recognition of oneself interacting with the world. The master has only an abstract relationship to the world. If the slave dies, the master is helpless; if the master dies, the slave is free. It is easy to see how for Marx the dialectic is a model for class conflict. The dialectic shows the importance of work. Working for a master is alienating and exploitative, but working for oneself is freedom. The only flaw in this picture is the focus on individuality. The master–slave dialectic is never simply between two individuals. It is always a social conflict involving many others, the past, laws, norms and so on. Marx more concretely recognizes this and makes the master–slave dialectic more real by situating it in human reality, in class struggle.

Nonetheless Hegel's master–slave dialectic brings into consciousness the importance of recognition from others and the centrality of labor in constructing the self. Individuality emerges as the process of socialization unfolds. Conflict can be useful but there are limits. At a certain point conflict just breaks people down: it does not build them up. No one today should have to fight to the death for recognition. One thing we all recognize is that the present world does not reflect who we are or who we want to be. Most of the constructed world was built on exploited labor and for the profit of the few. When you travel around your community, do your values and your sense of self, even your notion of your tribe, reflect back to you? Or do you see a world that is disconnected from you? Is our built world beautiful and embracing, or is it ugly and depressing? How many strip malls are near your home, how many stacked and crowded apartments are we stuffed into, how many tract homes fill our land, how many noisy roads with potholes run across your community? Our present world is conflicted, but so abstractly grasped that no one seems to know how to fix it. No one can quite grasp it such that we can change it.

11

The trolley problems mimic problems in our world. The world of the trolley problems is a dualistic and abstract world of tracks, levers, and anonymous individuals. People are separated, without face, and the options are paltry. It is a model of alienation and exploitation. When the trolley problems are presented, students constantly ask questions trying to fill in the situation or wanting more than two bad choices. But corresponding to our world, better options are not clearly available. We are told we must stay within the puzzle. But if the puzzle is too constraining for the richness of our humanness, then we should reject the puzzle and create a better one. And if our capitalist society is too constraining, too alienating and exploitative, for the richness of our humanness, then we should reject capitalist society and create a better society. Until we make our world reflect who we are both intrinsically and instrumentally, we will not have a reconciled world. Until the world reflects what we care about it will not be a meaningful world. Until we labor freely, recognize each other, and until our language, our laws, and our institutions recognize us all as free and equal, we will not have a good world. These things must be accomplished in reality. This is where Hegel gets close and yet falls short. His idealism tricks him into thinking that mind alone is enough. According to Hegel, as long as we recognize our own worth, we will be free. Anyone who has lived a little understands that only a philosopher could get this wrong. This is where philosophical sophistication runs into philosophical naïveté. This is where the philosopher automatically draws the trolley problem on the board, despite the fact that that the university has not updated the classroom in decades, and the whiteboard is now fifty shades of gray.

12

In the French film *Love Me If You Dare*, there is a Garden of Eden scene in which the two protagonists, when kids, metaphorically get thrown out of the Garden of Eden. The film reminds us that we all have been thrown out. The Garden of Eden moment corresponds to a time before the master–slave; it appeals to a sensibility before the age of alienation. But just like the fact that movies would be pretty boring if there were no conflict, human history makes sure the Garden of Eden phase is fleeting. In the film, Julian's mom is dying of cancer and his dad blames him. Sophie's situation is worse. She's an immigrant, poor and Polish, is getting teased by the French kids, and has to live in the depressing housing projects. She is proletarian, and Julian, with his wealthy but oppressive father, is bourgeois bred. Julian and Sophie don't want to join civilization, if this is civilization. They see how dark, phony, and ugly the world can be. They react against it by breaking the rules and inventing their own game. They dare each other to see what each is capable of. They share a pretty box to give the game meaning. It's a perverted game. They test each other; they test their loyalty, friendship, and love. They create their own world, their own version of the master–slave dialectic, but they cannot envision a way to transcend it. They take turns being the master and then the slave. Their own private game of master–slave protects them from the larger, unjust world where they are only slaves, and it makes the larger world pale in relation to their game of dare. They know the world is not capable of creating free human beings so they hold the idea, in a type of utopian Feuerbachian vision, inside their small tin box. Throughout the whole film they never open the box. It is only after they are hardened in cement that we get an alternative vision of them, in old age, with the can open so that they can pluck candy from it, let its beauty come out, and share it, in an utopian anti-ending. *Cap ou pas cap?*

13

Marx understood that capitalist society is not capable. And he asked why we accept the world as is. Why don't we strive for a Garden of Eden type world where we can also eat from the tree of knowledge? Of course, to become human we had to leave the garden of childhood and struggle in the realm of necessity. But from the fact that we struggle it doesn't have to follow that life cannot get better, that it should not get easier. Knowledge is a reflective action but it is not easy. Unlike in Garden of Eden myths, life is difficult, and actions take effort and are not always successful. Abstract beliefs and theoretical ideas separated from life don't have to prove themselves, so they will never be completely real or true. What's real and true exists as more than a belief, as more than a theory, and so it's hard to transcend the master–slave dialectic because it takes more than thought. Having to give up more than thoughts and ideas may make us stingy; people have trouble sharing the wealth, even when they know it's the right thing to do. But to get to the realm of freedom it is a necessity. Still, in our world, we have ideologically deluded ourselves into thinking we are fine within the realm of necessity. It's easier to simply say "that's just how the world is" rather than take uncertain action. But if we want more than animal existence, we have to take a chance.

Even in a barbaric world, it still seems risky to take a chance. Why? Well, those who are the masters potentially have a lot to lose. And it feels good being a master. And even the "slaves" buy into it, buy into the hope that one day their luck will change and they will become the masters. This vicious circle is why Marx said that when history repeats itself, the second time it is farce. But the longer we play this game, the more perverted, the more farcical, it becomes. Clearly, as capitalism advances it becomes more perverted. It infiltrates more and more areas of our existence. Every December it reaches another absurd pinnacle when consumerism reaffirms its vows to Christianity and they celebrate each other in an ever-widening carousel of gluttonous ingesting. Who knows, next season there may be a new video game where one can contemplate pushing Jesus onto the trolley tracks. Under what conditions would it be moral to push Jesus onto the tracks? And there must be some cases where it would be wrong. The traditional story that Jesus sacrificed for everyone makes the game too lame.

When we think about the trolley problems we can see the master–slave dialectic at work. Who really are the people hanging out at the trolley tracks? Who are the people forced to make uncomfortable decisions concerning people they don't even know? The dialectic outwits us here as we see it is the elite who are making decisions every day that affect numerous anonymous people in our world. Every day millions of us get run down by a trolley, in a manner of speaking. But we have to have empathy for those making decisions with nothing more to go by than abstract data and quantifiable numbers. Those at the tracks, holding tightly to the levers, did not set up this system. They found themselves in it, and as pretty much anyone else would do, they grabbed the powerful position that was right there waiting for them. We see time and time again how those who were initially without power gain power, and they end up doing the same thing that was done to them when they were vulnerable.

It is a systems problem. We need to have a better system, a system that serves all and gives power to all involved. We need to get rid of a system that puts some people in control and tells them to start pulling levers based on self-interest and abstract systems logic. We need a system where everyone controls the levers, a system that is based on cooperation, democracy, and the interests of everyone affected. We don't need Gods or supernatural beings mucking it up. Rather we need to talk to each other. Otherwise, as we have today, unaccountable people and abstract forces collude, and start pulling levers and pushing innocents, until the trickle down from it means unemployment for thousands, or lack of health insurance, or even death. We need to get rid of a system that has people at the bottom, down on the tracks, lined up like bowling pins, ready to be crushed by a sixteen-pound ball. And we need to get rid of a system that encourages people to become fat and diabetic before the age of ten, before they are even conscious of their fate. Every day we push our children onto the track of profit. We sacrifice them, their minds and bodies, and lives, to save the capitalist machine. Our children get run over; they get crushed, as a few get wealthier.

14

The Hegelian stages of history allow for a slightly different study of dialectics and offer a direct analysis of the end of history thesis. Stage one is un-differentiation and harmony. Individuals are not individuals yet. They don't sense a difference from others or from the group. This is the enfant stage where the child does not recognize itself as independent. Hold a small baby up to a mirror and it will not recognize itself. Yet there is a sense of harmony as this un-differentiation feels right, as there is no desire to separate. In this way a baby feels content, and at one with the mother or whoever it is closest to. Socially, primitive communist societies represent this. Historical stages in which private property rights don't yet exist and hierarchical titles such as Priest and Chief are still non-existent. This stage cannot last as our adolescent selves come out (whether our parents like it or not). We want to differentiate ourselves. We want freedom and individuality. Of course this causes disharmony. Socially speaking, slave, feudal, and capitalist societies capture this stage. The third and final stage is where we keep our differentiation but we get our harmony back. We are individuals who have become what we wanted to become, but now the world reflects it, accepts it and embraces it. My win is consistent with your win. It's the futile dream of every kid in college. Finish college, get a great job, and go back home for the holidays and celebrate with your parents as they respect the person you have become, and you respect and thank them for helping you get there. It's a lovely thought, but unfortunately most family get-togethers end more like *Home for the Holidays*.

The end of history thesis comes to a head in these Hegelian stages. The question is: Can capitalism and democracy, which look as if they belong in stage two, actually be modified to become stage three? In other words, can capitalism and democracy, if they become universal, give us differentiation and harmony? If the answer is yes, then Fukuyama's thesis will be vindicated both empirically and normatively. Capitalism and democracy will evolve into stage three where we will have differentiation (individual meaning) and harmony (individual meaning will connect with the community and world). We just need a kinder, gentler capitalism blended with democracy and it will happen. And then the end of history won't be so bad.

If the answer to the question of whether capitalism and democracy can give us differentiation and harmony is "no," then there are still two possibilities concerning the end of history. The first possibility is that stage three is a fiction. It's not consistent with human nature. If so, we are stuck with today's world. This is just as good as it gets, and we will keep on muddling through until we destroy ourselves. In this scenario capitalism and democracy will never lead to prosperity and global peace, so we will continue to fight each other, and some people and some nations will turn against modernity and embrace barbarism, medieval religious ideologies and so on. This is the nightmare scenario of the end of history thesis. Unfortunately, it seems not so unrealistic given the state of our world. But there is another possibility. The second possibility that follows from the inability of capitalism and democracy to lead to a stage-three style of differentiation and harmony is a scenario where we transcend capitalism and democracy. In other words, we reach the final stage of history, when, as Marx thought, we achieve and actualize a world of differentiation and harmony. Marx called this communism. Today we should call it democracy: it would be democracy. Democracy meaning that everyone affected has real power in the economic and political realms. This stage would consider everyone affected, it would consider all people. It would be the final stage. It would be the first stage of the realm of freedom.

15

This "final" stage of history, this realm of freedom, is beyond God and atheism. It is nothing but a human world where we make ourselves and those who matter proud. We are partly there already. Atheism is a viable belief today, so we have made progress. More and more of the modern world is rejecting regressive religion and reactionary atheism. Many people are closer to Marx than they would ever have imagined. Most people think Marx was a typical atheist, but his position is much more subtle than that. Marx said that when he hears people clinging to the word "atheism" it reminds him "of children, assuring everyone who is ready to listen to them that they are not afraid of the bogy man."[1] We can begin to see what he means by looking at his critique of Ludwig Feuerbach. Feuerbach, in *The Essence of Christianity*, tries to show that religion is a misinterpretation of human potential. According to Feuerbach, humans want virtue and are made for virtue. Justice, freedom, love, peace, and happiness are in us, and are what we could almost say, something we instinctively strive for. But the world is a pretty cold place and our utopian ideas don't easily materialize. The dialectic

---

1 Karl Marx, Letter to Ruge November 24, 1842 (https://www.marxists.org/archive/marx/works/subject/quotes/).

begins. Civilization and war have gone hand in hand. Our history is a violent history, yet civilization sustains and we have not given up the dream of a better world. Religion, which initially might have helped to keep the dream alive, has dialectically flipped as it has become conservative and works against a better world. When push comes to shove, the World's Religions have consistently sided with power. Grounded in the supernatural, religion cannot help but turn focus away from our concrete reality. The Feuerbachian point is that belief in God is a repressive belief that distracts from achieving a better world. Religion socializes people to feel dirty, worthless, and weak in the face of God. Religion teaches us that we are insignificant compared to God and so we have no right to question our fate. Religion, as a belief grounded in the supernatural, seeps down and corrupts our institutions, corrupts us, and prevents us from achieving what we are capable of achieving.

It is a sad story Feuerbach tells, for he says we did not invent religion out of fear or self-hate, but rather that we invented God to hold on to our dearest humanistic values for us, to keep the Hegelian stage three coherent until the time we could transition to stage three. But we have gotten amnesia and have forgotten that we are the authors of God and religious belief. And it gets worse, because now we are alienated from our own values, and they look down at us, through our idea of God, and make us feel weaker than we are and less than we can be. Feuerbach blames religion for much of the human misery and suffering in the world. What nature doesn't take from us, religion does. Feuerbach thinks we need to reject religion and claim the heavenly values for ourselves. We, as a people, are God. We, meaning humanity, are moving toward omnipotence, omniscience, and omnibenevolence. It's a beautiful image of human nature and human potential. We really are good; we just lost our way. Change your ideas and you can change your life. It would play well as a Sunday morning infomercial.

Feuerbach puts belief at the center of his analysis and so gives priority to idealism as he blames religion for social injustice, apathy, and ideological distortion. Marx has a more nuanced view. He sees religion as a symptom of the problem, not the cause of the problem. Marx is a materialist but not a traditional one. He does not think there is some material foundation, some metaphysical materialism that will provide a foundation for humans. Rather his materialism is a philosophy of collective action. We are historical and biological creatures who actively construct our world, and we create the world and knowledge through our collective practices. There is no bedrock foundation, no thing-in-itself, in either an idealist or materialist sense. There is simply constant, dialectical interplay between subjects and a world we are always already part of. Who we are is both a product of history and biology, and biology is always in history, and history is always of a biological creature.

We may analytically separate them out, but that is an intellectual exercise and a differentiation we make, the world doesn't analytically separate biology and history. Just as we can analytically separate out parts of ourselves, both, mental and physical, and the characteristics, qualities, beliefs, actions, drives, and so on that make us who we are, we cannot literally separate ourselves. We are always already part of ourselves and are ourselves. There is no bedrock foundation, either spiritually or materially, over us or under us, we are just us, and we are constantly active until the moment of our death.

If our interactions, and especially our material interactions, create the world and our knowledge of the world, then religious belief is just a symptom rather than a cause of who we are and what our world means. Religion cannot be blamed or praised for the state of the world. "Religious suffering is at the same time the expression of real suffering and also the protest against real suffering. Religion is the sigh of the oppressed creature, the sentiment of a heartless world, and the soul of soulless conditions. It is the opium of the people."[1] In other words religion is not the cause of human misery or the solution to human misery. But it is a symptom of what is wrong and a peek into what is right. It both reflects and rationalizes our practices, and as such it should be analyzed in relation to our material interactions. For Marx, this starts with labor.

16

Human labor is unique in that productivity and efficiency tend to increase over time; we produce more than we need both quantitatively and qualitatively. Marx calls the former variety. We create tools and techniques that make our work easier, more efficient, more environmentally sound, and more fun. It's more complicated than this. Labor does get better and worse as we lose the ability — hipsters notwithstanding — to labor without technology. The latter we call surplus and this really has two meanings. First, we can produce beyond our immediate needs; second, we can produce so we don't have to work tomorrow. Surplus allows us freedom to do other things. The other meaning of surplus is an aesthetic meaning. We don't just make things — we prefer to make them beautiful. We want useful things, but we also want them to look good. We want to see ourselves in our creations, such that artifacts seem as if they are works of art, and sometimes they even become works of art. The superstructure reflects and distorts the manner in which our labor is organized such that one can say that our deepest values are hidden in the super-structural apparatus, in beliefs including religion.

---

1 Marx, Contribution to the Critique of Hegel's Philosophy of Right: Introduction, in *The Marx–Engels Reader*, p. 54.

Religion, like other aspects of the superstructure, reflects and distorts. It reflects economic truth, and it distorts or hides the contradictions within our economy. It softens the blow of our material world by offering a promise of happiness. From a Hegelian–Marxist perspective we could talk about sports as part of the superstructure. To just paint a picture, an artistic representation, we could say that it begins with soccer. Soccer reflects the values of a society grounded in agriculture. It reflects a world where bodies must be strong, light, fleet of foot, agile, and with technical skill. In this world everybody gets to kick the ball, everybody knows how things operate. If the father dies, the mother and children can take over his job on the farm. Everybody can do everything. As society "advances," and the division of labor increases, and cottage industries and new technologies develop, baseball becomes the sport of choice. Baseball has more specialization; everyone has a position, but the pitcher and catcher control the ball. Class distinctions are growing. Still, everyone gets a chance at bat, and every team must follow the rotation. Then with the advent of the factory, of manufacturing, arises American football. Football produces big, strong bodies, bodies that can push things around, lift heavy things, can work as a team, and it has a robust division of labor, an offense and a defense, and special teams. In the factory there are many roles, some more important than others: the assembly line, the supervisors, the truckers, the loaders and unloaders, the tool makers and die casters, and such. But just as most football players are anonymous helmets trying to move the line of scrimmage, most workers are cogs in the machine. When one gets hurt, it's next man up. But the quarterback is granted a special and higher role. The quarterback is the shop manager, and of course, there are many above him.

As we move into the postmodern world, the information age, with technology, the demise of unions, and the need for flexibility, we get basketball. Basketball is a fluid, fast, ever-changing sport. There is constant scoring, the bodies are long, defined, and have aesthetic virtue. They fly through the air and dunk, block, steal, pass, shoot the three, trap, dribble, and assist. They wear shorts and tank tops to show off the body; it's an aesthetic sport that highlights the beauty of the human body in motion. It is dangerous though because the aesthetics mask the deeper economic truth. The image begins to define the exchange value ("be like Mike" and "it's all about the shoes") and both image and exchange takes precedence over use value. As technology takes us even deeper into and down the rabbit hole, things such as computer gaming become sports and become means to make money. This reflects our stagnant, virtual world. A couch potato can now be an athlete and can find material success. Get good at video games and maybe you can pilot a drone. You can kill people halfway around the world while sitting on your couch. This connects with the other growing sport — MMA. Dana White claims that mixed martial arts, and the UFC in particular, is the fastest growing sport today. Whether literally true or not, White makes a point as this sport captures the dialectic between war and civilization that is our world today. We pride ourselves as W. said as "a peace loving nation," but in reality we are a contested and conflicted class society, and a techno-warrior nation. We use poor people and drones to fight our battles. We have hundreds of military bases across the globe. Sports reflect and rationalize this world and yet also offer a promise of happiness beyond the present.

17

Sport, today, is an entertainment business, a funhouse amusement center. Sport was not always about money and entertainment. For the Greeks sport was more directly linked to their base, to who they were explicitly. In the ancient world sport was self-consciously preparation for warfare; it was battle oriented. As stylized it had an aesthetic element and a sports-like competitive element, but everyone knew sport was directly related to the skills needed to survive and to dominate in battle. The Ancient Greeks were warriors and their sports acknowledged that truth. Sport then was not mere entertainment or distraction. The ancients even honored their dead by integrating sports into funerals. Funeral games were athletic events which honored the dead and kept those alive better prepared for future battles. Contrast that with today where sports are becoming more and more absurd. Shows such as American Gladiator or Ninja Warrior are spectacles that make the human spirit worse. They are distracting entertainment meant to keep us on the couch and glued to the television set. Today sports are a business built to exploit everyone it touches. Sports reflect how ideological our society has become. Sport is a tool to manipulate its own population: it exploits the athletes and it seduces the consumers. We waste our lives following athletic events that have become meaningless. From the Super Bowl to March Madness, to the NBA Finals and the World Series, it is now all about money, and the human meaning and value has been completely eclipsed.

Gambling has taken center stage with sports. From fantasy leagues to the tracks, to the office March Madness pool, and even in Pop Warner Football, sports don't exist in America without gambling. Our brand of capitalism is just one big Vegas-style casino. The system runs by an irrational, betting, stock market-style logic that is unhealthy and unethical. And it doesn't work for sports or the economy. If you doubt this you have a very short memory. Bush's final act, signifying nothing, was to leave office right after the collapse of the American economy, the popping of the housing bubble, the failure of the big banks, and the tanking of the stock market. His military shenanigans distracted us while they made his class richer and made the rest of us less safe. He treated the White House as a sporting team and only cared about his win. The American people lost. From the falling of the towers to the falling of the stock market, it was the average American who fell with them. But since the house never loses, Washington bailed out the banks and those "holding the bank."

And to think some of us were naïve enough to think Bush's first act of allowing the towers to fall would be his worst mistake, his most selfish act of not protecting the country. He started his administration by letting the towers fall and ended it by helping the markets crash. But like any cheat, he claims innocence till the end, despite the facts, despite the material evidence. We should have known. We should have looked more closely at the superstructure. George W. Bush's favorite activity, his sport, is bicycling, just like Lance Armstrong.

18

This is why we can't allow a family, a class, or any unaccountable segment of the population to control the trolley, to control the White House. Irresponsibility, exploitation, and horrible consequences will follow. While we can see the inner meaning of our society by looking at the superstructure, we need only look at the day-to-day working conditions of most Americans to see and feel the alienation. Capitalism has improved labor's efficiency quite a bit, but one salient area where it falls short is in the area of alienation. In the *1844 Manuscripts* Marx concretizes Hegel and shows four interrelated types of alienation: alienation from the object, activity, others, and the Species. Ask yourself if this model still holds validity. Alienation from the product means that what workers create at work stands outside and above them as workers. Workers do not have control over the product so they cannot put themselves into their labor in a way that will reflect back to them. Even owners view their products through the lens of making money, from the profit incentive. Activity too is structured to be alienating. Activity is assembly-line like, not only in the factory, but even when "enjoying a meal" at Subway and Starbucks. Even in our leisure activities, such as going to amusement parks, we are herded like cattle around the farm.

Further, we are alienated from each other. It's a cutthroat world where you take a risk being honest or authentic to your fellow workers, to consumers, or supervisors. Honesty, community, and putting others first are not how the game is played, and it certainly is not in one's interest in the current system. If you can push the fat man, you push the fat man. Finally, we experience alienation from our Species-Being — from Humanity. This is rather abstract, but the point is, linking with Feuerbach, that our humanistic selves and our desire to see future generations thrive have become secondary preoccupations.

Marx believes his theory of alienation shows us concretely where and how our labor is lacking and what "communism" would look like, at least philosophically. He leaves it to us to fill in the details, but by pointing out the areas that fall short of our better virtues he shows us the direction that will overcome the deficits. Those affected must have a direct say, have control, of the product and activity of labor. Also, our relations with each other must be democratic, and our world should reflect us. Having less control, less free activity, more irrational competition, and further ignoring our virtues and humanity will not fix anything. Overcoming alienation and eliminating disharmony, while cultivating creativity and individuality, is his vision. When these are accomplished, when they are actualized, interest in God and atheism will fade away. When the eclipse retreats, our ideas and our practices will come together as we make ourselves and others proud, as they make themselves and us proud. There will be no need or interest in transcending or denigrating our world. In a world that reflects us there will be no separation between the different players in the trolley problems, for the idea of sacrificing some for the sake of others would not exist. Either we all sacrifice or none of us will. Students, when discussing the puzzles, often ask if they can throw themselves in front of the trolley rather than let someone else be the victim. The fact that this question pops into so many young minds may signal that Feuerbach's claim that God is simply a projection of our best humanity is true.

19

The true dialectic then is the one between seeing the world as our practical creation and forgetting this fact. In Lukácsian terms it is the dialectic between self-recognition and reification. Overcoming the dualism requires self-recognition in all aspects of reality, and it starts with the economy. The mode of production, including both the relations and forces of production, are the base; they are our practical creation, and as the heart of social labor they are the dominant side of the dialectic. When we forget that the economy is nothing but women and men working to reproduce our world, when we forget that the market is not a thing but is simply a name for the way we have chosen to organize our labor — when we forget this, we have fallen victim to reification.

Language easily distorts the continuity of the world as it prefers dualisms and separation. Language has the propensity to be metaphysical. Nietzsche detailed the way language congeals becoming into the appearance of being.

The language of "the self" makes it seem as if there is an essential self under all the actions that create a self. And Nietzsche's famous example pointing out that the words "lightning strikes" makes it sound as though there is this thing called lightning that is going to strike, makes this point. But just as the self is nothing but the sum of what one does, lightning just is the strike. There is no agent or doer hiding, just waiting to strike. Nietzsche recognized that God is like grammar. "I fear we are not getting rid of God because we still believe in grammar."[1] God and grammar have been useful for structuring aspects of human life, but they don't exist outside us. Still, we tend to think they do. Both are abstractions we created to make sense of the world and ourselves. God was useful, perhaps, until the seventeenth century, and grammar is still vital, although the new texting "language" is shifting things. In any case, grammar is a bigger god than God. We can live complete human lives without ever invoking supernatural beings, but we need language to be fully human, and language does need some sort of structure. We can value both — God for being there when it was helpful for us, for making the world more intelligible for a spell — and grammar for making language more communicative. Yet both God and grammar have the propensity to think they are bigger than they are. The priest and the grammarian fetishize their objects and risk spoiling their truth and true beauty as historical sidekicks. God we simply made up to structure our lives; and grammar we simply made up to structure our language. Yet God is often used to crush and dismiss others and grammar is often used to mock and discount others. In this way we can say grammar is the language of God.

20

The model here is Feuerbach's critique of religion. Humans created God. Humans created grammar. Humans created the market. Now, like God, more human creations stand above us and control us as we forget they are our creations and we forget that we can change and alter them as we find necessary. Self-recognition is difficult and will only be complete through reflective, conscious actions. But language again tries to trick us. The free market is comparable to free will, a term that easily lends itself to reification. There is no such thing, outside us or in us, called free will. We just will; and as we grow, as we learn to control our actions and thoughts, as we learn to distinguish the inner from the outer, we develop the ability to better control ourselves and the world we are part of. Willing is a talent; we can either cultivate or lose the skill. It is part of a larger process, but is not an independent thing. Free will is not free. It is regulated and comes from us, our history, our biology, our reasons, desires, and needs. This is not bad

1 Nietzsche, *Twilight of the Idols*, p. 48.

and it does not make it unfree. If willing didn't come out of a history then it would just be random. Randomness is not freedom.

And it's the same with the so-called free market. There is no free market in nature. There is no market in nature. There is no market without society, and there is no society without structure, constraints, rules, and regulations. Government did not intrude onto some natural free market existing before us; governments just regulate and maintain what we created. We created a society with laws and norms and set the terms and limits of our economic interactions from the start. In this way there has always been regulation and constraints on what can and cannot be done. It is not a question of a free vs. unfree market. It is a question of what regulations and constraints we accept and which we do not accept. It is a question of the type of market we want to create. Without rules the market would not be free, it would be random and arbitrary, and that's not freedom. But democratic decision-making would be free. I wonder why free-marketers are against that. Today it is popular to claim: "freedom is not free," but really it is the market that never was and never could be "free."

21

As we must fundamentally satisfy our biological and material needs in order to survive, they get labeled the base, and as our language, norms, and laws become more explicit, as we have evolved from less than human to linguistic creatures, the state sits just above the base. The dialectic works here in a manner we are all very familiar with. As the political slogan said "It's the economy stupid." Politics is fed by the economic interests, and works on behalf and at the behest of the most powerful economic forces in society. This is not news to anyone today. If you or I want to talk to Obama he probably won't answer our phone call, but Bill Gates and Warren Buffett he will. Still, the state is its own power, and exists in dialectical tension, as well as harmony, concerning the base. Both always already exist in a human world, but there is not complete symmetry since survival underwrites history's march. Yet as historical beings survival needs too are intertwined with the political. We can never start again, or get to a moment before politics. Everything is political and even if we fell into a post-apocalyptic world it would still be a political one, cobbled together from our political past, as much as our labor and survival would be the same.

The superstructure then dialectically works with both the state and the base. As closest to Plato's forms, as ideas, the superstructure is the highest and the lowest. It is highest because it takes all that is human and articulates it in theoretical language, and develops leisure vocations such as philosophy, religion, sports, and art. As a higher realm the superstructure allows us to develop and even acquire a deeper freedom than we can at the base, as the former is not all about efficiency, outputs, and productivity. It is the sublime extra that makes human life worth living. Still, it is dialectically married to the state and base, to history, and arises from all of it, and so will be as contradictory as it is consistent, it will be as much material as it is idea, it will continue to be instrumental even as it is intrinsic. Even as idea the superstructure cannot delink from the rest of society, so as theory forgets its intertwinement with practice it becomes, not a pure Platonic form, but rather it becomes pure ideology. As misunderstood purity, theory misunderstands the world and itself.

22

As Marx tried to demystify the world, his focus turned to a very specific concept distorting the modern mind. It is not God that is the great trickster, rather it is something much more innocuous sounding — it is the commodity. What is a commodity? It's something made to be sold on the market. In the modern world the commodity form is the most telling hieroglyphic within the dialectic of reification and self-recognition. We think of a commodity as a thing because it is a thing. But we must get under this immediacy to the human processes that created it and that put our mark into it. A commodity is a product of human labor, so the trick is to see ourselves in the commodity if we really want to know it, if we really want to know ourselves. There are no commodities without the human, and we could create a world without commodities. We recognize that commodities are useful, and that we live in a system where we exchange useful things. All objects have use value, as all objects have qualities to them that are good for something. But objects that are also commodities have exchange value too. Of course it starts with use value. Everything is useful for something. The usefulness depends on the qualities within the object, mediated with our needs and interests. Whereas use value is in the object, is material, exchange value is, so to speak, in us, is relational, is an idea or value that comes out of material production. We have created a society where we exchange goods and services and we have created a system of exchange. There is no free market or free exchange outside us. We could give things away for free, we could abolish all laws, we could legalize stealing, or we could just steal, but that would still be a system we are propagating and so not free or unregulated. A system where there is no government would have to be regulated, so that we all follow the so-called non-rules. And if we wanted no government and decided that each would regulate for themselves that's still a political decision. Not having rules is a rule; it is not somehow free, natural, and unregulated.

This is where you see the manipulation of corporate America aimed at individuals wanting to own their own business. It is one aspect of "the American dream" to own one's own business. Unlike corporate America, most Americans don't dream of having an army of wage-laborers doing their work. Rather most Americans dream of doing the work themselves and owning their business. The irony is that this is communism. Communism is where the workers own the means of production. Small businesses, where individuals and their families own and work at the business, is the model of communism. It is only because of the logic of capitalism — grow or die — that many expand and build up their business. It's often just a survival technique. Sole proprietorships are mini-communist utopias.

The Marxist point (and the capitalist Adam Smith's point, too), though, is that we do not determine exchange based on the qualities within objects, rather we base exchange on the labor we put into objects. A fair exchange would be one in which one person exchanges something of equal labor with another of equal labor. If it took a competent person two hours to whittle a wazoo and it took another competent person four hours to pick a bushel of apples, a fair exchange would be to trade two wazoos for the bushel of apples.

Money makes exchange easier but it also is an abstraction from direct exchange, and as such, it makes it easier to cheat on exchange. At this point in our modern economy the ability to figure out what a fair exchange is seems hopeless. Still, theoretically it should be possible. But most of us just feel as if we got a fair deal when the price seems right given what we know about what things cost or should cost. In other words we really don't have any sense of the real value that was created by the labor. In this way, the things we buy, commodities, turn into fetishes. We just act as if the value is in the object, in the commodity. But's it not. The value was created because of human labor. As we forget this it makes it easier to care more for things than for people.

If in modernity the point is to have justice and freedom for all, then one might wonder where the idea of profit fits. When we are exchanging things freely there should be no profit. I give you what you deserve and you give me back what I deserve. That would be treating each other as free and equal human beings. Why would we not want this to be the model for interacting with others? The alternative is using others, as in the ring of Gyges. And yet almost all of us work really hard, while some end up with much more than the others. Is it really because they are working harder? Do you seriously think those who have more are objectively creating more value? Or has the system determined that their labor has more value? Is picking up garbage really less valuable than doing breast augmentation? Is it possible that the current system favors and rewards some ways of creating value more than others, and that this has nothing to do with use or exchange value? Do you think that those trading stocks on Wall Street are doing something more useful and something that requires more labor than most other jobs? What is really going on?

According to Marx the major reason we do not have a free system is because of wage labor. Capitalism is a system dependent on class distinctions, dependent on owners and workers interacting in undemocratic ways. Workers work for a wage rather than getting paid the value they create. All of us who have jobs see right away that we don't get paid the value we create. Rather we get a wage, sometimes a nice wage, but the owners take some of the value we create for themselves. They justify it by saying things such as they take all the risk. What risk? If things go badly, it's the workers who suffer in lower wages or even losing their jobs. If things go really badly, capitalists simply lose the business and become workers. So what's the risk? If workers don't take risks, what's the risk of capitalists becoming workers? Donald Trump's businesses have filed bankruptcy many times. Is he really taking more risks than the rest of us, if the system allows him that privilege? Did he really risk anything? Was the market really free? The answers are too obvious to even debate.

If people are so deluded that they think General Motors or Donald Trump take a bigger risk than anyone else trying to survive, week to week, they are being willfully ignorant. The government bailed out General Motors. Did the government bail you out? Did it help most working Americans when their houses' values dropped, when they went underwater, when their stocks became worthless?

The philosophical point here is that we have created a system with exploitation built into it, but we have been fed beliefs, from the time we were young, that make it very difficult to see the exploitation. The promise of modernity, the promise of life, liberty, and the pursuit of happiness, according to Marx, is a false belief — if it is predicated on a capitalist system wedded to alienation and exploitation. Capitalism is better than slavery, feudalism, and state communism, but still, according to its own internal logic, wage-labor, it is exploitative. If capitalism cannot be critiqued or challenged, then we are conceding that the end of history, the best we can do, is to continue to exploit and alienate. One must wonder why people so ruthlessly insist on defending a system that treats most people as commodities, treats most people as things, as objects, to be bought and sold, and then tossed away when their use value has been all used up. Whose interest do you think this serves?

23

The belief in God and the belief in atheism are reified ideas and commodified products supporting an exploitative industry and rationalizing an alienating world. As the idea that even humans are commodities has become common sense, we can see the effect on the superstructure. Religion, culture, sports, and the arts are now driven by the commodity form. The artifacts, congregations, the events, the spectators, youth groups, the actors, the players, the priests, and the artists are commodities, as culture has become what Horkheimer and Adorno labeled "the culture industry." The world is run by money, is about money, as the logic of business has become ubiquitous. One can even imagine a new television show next season: *The Trolley Problems*. In this show we can have people from across the country put into various trolley-problem type situations and we can phone in and bet on who will push the fat man, who will pull the lever, and so on. We can have office pools and fantasy leagues to increase the fun. Done correctly, I'm sure, even a philosophy puzzle can become a hit, and make a few people rich. Meanwhile the rest keep getting pushed and run over, as democratic values get completely eclipsed, and the end of history thesis celebrates itself in a festival of insignificance.

CHAPTER 5. SARTRE THE IMMORTAL

1

Nick Bostrom's book *Superintelligence*, written for the futuristic dreamer, was a best seller, proving that the metaphysical urge is still alive and well. Bostrom's a philosopher who early on was shaped by existential philosophy, the likes of Schopenhauer and Nietzsche, but he came to see them as outdated and traded in his humanism for a version of transhumanism. If only it were that simple, bad faith would be extinct. The transhumanist faithful look to the future and dream of immortality. Where an existentialist strives to live in the present, a transhumanist projects into the future at the expense of the present; one must wonder if the expense is worth it: living on a different continent than one's wife and child, chewing nicotine gum, downing gallons of coffee and super-shakes, popping Modafinil and such in the desire to enhance cognition and stave off death.[1] Living in frenzy, in the name of a distant future, is the surest way not to suck the marrow out of the present. It is a life living for a belief, not unlike a traditional religion. The Singularity crowd has its answer to Nietzsche's non-question question: "Are we God's mistake, or is God our mistake?" For Bostrom it is both. First, we are about to make the mistake of creating God, and then this God will eliminate us. Bostrom is seriously worried that we will create an AI version of the Übermensch which will in turn discard us as if we were nothing but an annoying pest. At best, we will end up no better than Voltaire's rats on

---

1 Raffi Khatchadourian, "The Doomsday Invention" (*The New Yorker*, November 23, 2015).

the ship, while that super-intelligent AI captain steers its way throughout the universe.

2

Jean-Paul Sartre (whose UFC name would be JPS) would wonder what the point of living forever is if you never experience life as lived, deeply lived, with no thought of metaphysical transcendence. Can the question of whether Humanity will become transcendent or perish be a central question for an existentialist? Worrying about the existential threat of Humanity after studying existentialism is like worrying about how God will punish you after the death of God. Humanity is not eternal, and even if it were, that would be no more than a distraction for mortal individuals. And if an individual could somehow achieve immortality, one would become many selves over the course of forever. Rather than dying once, the immortal ones, when they lose the sense (the form) of their latest former self, would die an infinite number of times; with the result being a numbing of the very essence of what it means to be human, or, alternatively, living eternal misery. It doesn't take an AI to destroy humanistic values. Even if we started recording all our lives, as some of the new generation last men who call themselves Nietzschean do, and so held all the content of our existence present-at-hand and ready-to-hand, we would lose our form, as quantity transforms into un-quality. With the change in form so goes the self before the change and in whose name the dream lived.

In any case, today's immortality seekers have reopened the metaphysical urge in a new portal, but when you pour old wine into new bottles, the drink becomes spoiled. A good wine only ages well once and cannot survive a transplant. The individual bottle need not care that pinot noir will not last forever and an individual need not care that humanity is ultimately ephemeral. And just as a bottle opened too soon, or too late, loses its sublime essence, Individuals will lose their sublime essence if their lives are taken too quickly or if they carry on too long. Forever would be too long. We can either uncork our lives and drink up, or freak out over the fact that one day everything we know and care about, including ourselves, will be erased so thoroughly that no trace will be left behind. Present consciousness matters, the bottle is open, it must be drunk, must be finished. As they say in Mauritius when they finish a bottle of wine — Un homme est mort.

3

Rather than enjoying the show one is starring in, the metaphysical urge encourages the hopefuls to get drunk with worry over the day the show will be canceled. They all eventually end, often not soon enough, and one day the television will be gone as our world will be, regardless of whether the human comedy is still playing. Existentialism warns against this type of abstraction, stories that see life as a story, and stories that only seem worthwhile if there's a happy ending. Life has no happy ending and life is not a story. Still, concrete human life offers meaning and redemption, even as it is necessarily tragic.

As so called pro-lifers fetishize the fetus, those who opt for cryonetics we might call "self pro-lifers." But within their self-fetish we see a contradiction curled into the fetal position within the name transhumanism itself — a contradiction contained within the very term they self-identify with. Only if lightning could first hide and then strike at will could a human first freeze and then transcend at will. But if lightning just is the strike, then to be human just is to transcend. If there is change that sustains consciousness, then we have not transcended the human, for to be human is to sustain consciousness. If we have change and lose consciousness, then the age of the human is over. Transhumanism is just another name for death. Fear of AI is a religious fear.

Compared to other transhumanists, or Singularity types, it's hard to tell if Bostrom is a better player than we have seen before or if it's just that the immortality game has changed. Steph Curry is an amazing basketball player, to say the least, but we cannot separate what he can do on the basketball court from the way the game has changed. In today's game players get to "unofficially" palm the ball, travel, switch pivot, and the defenders have all kinds of new restrictions imposed upon them. The game is different than it was even five or ten years ago, and radically different than forty or fifty years ago; Curry's greatness needs to be understood within this context. Still, we can say his game is something different from, and in some ways superior, to what we have seen. Likewise those who worry about AI, and those who want to transcend humanity, or capture the singularity, are playing the same God/atheism game but with new rules, so we need to analyze the context. The rules have changed because technology has advanced incredibly quickly, and so it seems like a new game or at least a more exciting game. Today's basketball game gives those who were not moved by the slow pace and whiteness of basketball before 1950 something to get excited about. But if we calm our fears and step back from the flashy action, we see that it is fundamentally still the same; the game of being human goes on but with new players, wearing new brands of shoes, with new gadgets, each trying to leave his mark. It's Steph Curry's chance to shine, Kobe is done, and we will never see Magic, or Michael, or Pistol Pete on the court again. They all had their moment and they did what they did. Now we are on the court and AI is a new rule. It's on the court with us, and it needs to be re-centered into human discussions about existence without becoming metaphysical.

We could accept Bostrom's fears and admit that AI could adapt to the rules and then create new rules and take over the game. Before we realize what's happening, the AI could rig things so we cannot turn it off, and next thing we know it's controlling us rather than us it. And if the AI is significantly more intelligent than we are, this seems perfectly plausible. And AI will develop driven by human's (apparently Google's) instrumental goals, so its programming will probably prompt it to predict and control the world rather than intrinsically understand it. But who knows. Many of us reject our programming. The new AI might find itself navigating the sea of the universe as a new Odysseus. As Odysseus, AI may want to experience the intrinsic beauty of the Sirens but also want to "live." Would AI avoid the Sirens' island altogether or sail past beauty while plugging our ears, or will it, perhaps, let us all join in the sublime moment until we crash onto the rocks? If programs or people are too intrinsically focused or too instrumentally motivated, they could lose their selves and drown in the sea. AI, like humans obsessed with survival, may run the danger of being too instrumental. On the other hand, if the AI has no human conception of self, perhaps it won't be concerned with self-preservation and will evolve in a radically intrinsic way. Perhaps it will only care about truth, beauty, and justice, and will seize itself as a living entity. Or maybe it won't care about anything at all.

In any case, humans and potentially conscious and reflective non-humans run the risk of misinterpreting existence, especially if they do not recognize that they are always already interpreting. A philosopher studying "Existential Risk" may be living existential avoidance behavior. It might be more rational to pay a psychologist to help one figure out why one is so afraid of death rather than giving Alcor all that cash. And it is about cash. Today we have a marriage of science and artificial intelligence, and the priest performing the ceremony is capitalism. Together they are being funded and directed by economic factors. The tech industry is all about AI now, and the best and brightest in it are embracing industry over academia. And, of course, between the corporations and the government, we know what will happen to and with this technology — Oppenheimer's return as farce. While the transhumanists dream of individual consciousness merging into a cyber-soup, those of us not floating in this lukewarm pot can see on the bottom of the cup a Buddha stamp announcing "Made in China" and the Campbell's logo next to it. One should be very careful about trading in existentialist philosophy for the newest fad. Rejecting nineteenth-century German philosophers for futurism is a living, hellish eschatology well-earned.

4

John-Paul Sartre's existentialist philosophy is a philosophy of action. It is a philosophy he lived. As lived it transcends God and atheism. As written, his philosophy does too, but that is more difficult to see. Compared to most of the philosophy written in the 20th century, Jean-Paul Sartre's celebrated lecture "Existentialism is a Humanism" is a deceptively easy read. Perhaps too easy. Today, based on this text, too many underestimate the depth of Sartre's existentialism. The essay emphasizes freedom and Sartre's atheism, but his philosophy has many more important layers to it. For instance, while it is true that Sartre makes it abundantly clear that he is an atheist, his atheism is deeper and more subtle than the loud atheist philosophers writing today. Likewise, his defense of freedom is based on sophisticated philosophical arguments and not pessimistic — yet chic —French views on freedom, or clever— yet runaway — American compatibilist theory. Rather Sartre's philosophy is chock full of optimistic philosophical insights and relevant, real-life situations.

A good starting point for these insights and situations is the text *Existentialism and Human Emotions*. This book is sufficient to trace Sartre's path beyond God and atheism. It starts with the essay "Existentialism is a Humanism" and the attack on existentialism from both Christians and Communists. We can see Sartre's response to each as a concrete refutation of the abstract ideas of God and atheism, and, as such, we can read Sartre as going beyond God and atheism through his refutation of both Christianity and actual existing Communism. In other words, the God/atheist dialectic is an abstraction of the Christian/Communist dialectic. We will see that, from Sartre's perspective, both of these ideologies underemphasize the ontological and epistemological truth of an active, knowing subject, and so both fall victim to reification. Further, in a surprising twist (for one accused of nihilism), we will see that Sartre's philosophy is Hegelian in so far as it pushes the atheist/God dialectic until it synthesizes them, so to speak, into something essentially greater. As greater, truth begins to emerge to the extent that quantity transforms into quality, to the extent that it resolves the theory/practice split into concrete, enlightened action.

5

Those who doubt that quantity can transform into quality only need to look at the coaching brilliance of Clyde Hart. Hart has trained the greatest 400-meter runners in history. His training methods and philosophy are unique, and despite the success, still not adequately respected by the greater track and field community. Sprinters are traditionally taught that they must consistently train fast, that it is better to train short to long, meaning in the beginning of the season run short distances as fast as possible and build outward to longer distances. Hart does the opposite. He trains long to short. At the beginning of the season his athletes run longer distances, and repeats, at a slower pace than traditional sprinter workouts. Then, as the season progresses, Hart shortens the distances and the repeats, but rarely has his sprinters running all out. He came to this philosophy accidently. His athletes were getting injured, pulling muscles and so on. Increasing the quantity, and running slower, kept his athletes healthy and gave them a strength and endurance base for important races later in the season. His quantitative training produced qualitative results, as when Michael Johnson broke world records in the 200 meters and 400 meters and won gold medals in both events during the same Olympic year. This is almost unheard of in those events.

JPS is like Clyde Hart. He invented a new training program in philosophy. He invented existentialism (in the same quasi-inventive way that Hart invented long to short) and proved that through a sufficient quantity of freely chosen actions one can qualitatively change himself and make himself and those who matter proud. The training starts with a critique of the reified beliefs and immature identities of actually existing Christianity and Communism.

The Christian critique of existentialism equates existentialism with a deficiency of morality. The Communist critique equates existentialism with a naïve individualistic view of the human. The Christian assumes that you need God to have morality. In fact, most Christians in America still believe an atheist is by definition immoral, and atheists are always ranked as one of the most hated groups in this country. The communist, similar to today's science-minded atheist, has little patience for existentialism. Both the communist and the scientist are less concerned with the individual than with the group, the theory, or the type and both question existentialism's radical view of freedom. The point here is that today the average Christian and the average atheist are not inclined toward existentialism, and most likely have not even heard of the term, let alone understood it.

The communist values solidarity, and without God to unify, communists turn to the party to fill the gap created by their atheism. The idea is that without God people will turn to each other. Humanity replaces God. But Sartre's existentialism rejects this move. According to Sartre, when one gets rid of God, it makes no sense to replace God with an inferior substitute. Without God there is no "big Other" to fill that gap. Rather than search for a substitute Sartre rejects the game itself. Communists don't understand this so they accuse him of a type of "desperate quietism."[1] Existentialism denies final answers and is centered on the individual, and for French Communist thought this meant existentialists were rejecting their values. But Sartre is rejecting only the foundation of their values; he rejects the idea that Marxism is a science, a necessity, or a panacea. He does not reject Marx or communistic values, but he understands they are contingent choices that can be only actualized through freely chosen actions. Sartre today probably would engage with the new forms of identity politics and fight with them while at the same time trying to keep the non-foundational truths of existentialism in the foreground. The new social movements offer new possibilities for freedom and individuality yet can tend toward paternalism. We must be careful to understand what is at stake when we advocate for things such as trigger warnings and safe spots. An existentialist perspective would look at these concretely and ask if they are making spaces to grow individuality and freedom, if they are promoting freely chosen actions, or if they are denying these values to the individuals concerned. Context will answer these questions. Sartre saw within the French Communist Party of his day the tendency to replace one authority figure with another. After the death of God the only answer in politics is democracy, and democracy that is accountable to all subjects and that includes all subjects. Neither the party nor the movement stands above concrete individuals. Nothing stands above dialogue. As such, the questions and critiques Sartre brings to consciousness do not reduce his philosophy to a philosophy of contemplation or a "bourgeois" philosophy for the elite.

6

The second critique, the religious one, is dressed up as a moral critique but it is really a metaphysical one. It accuses existentialism of "dwelling on human degradation"[2] and "neglecting the gracious and beautiful, the bright side of human nature." This is a Christian critique that finds the idea of existentialism unholy both in regards to its supposedly vulgar content and to its form. The form of Existentialism is a thinking–acting subject forced to create and interpret. This replaces the God-form, and so the Christian assumes that with the death of God life will have no meaning. Christians think that life without God loses its form and empties its content. For Christians, the worry is that without God there are no commandments that must be followed, "anything is permissible" and life becomes subject to an individual's caprice, with the result being a shallow pleasure-seeking

1 Sartre, *Existentialism and Human Emotions*, p. 9.
2 All my quotations in this section from Sartre are from *Existentialism and Human Emotions*, pp. 9–12.

life. Christians are undoubtedly also worried about losing the ability (and privilege) of condemning the views and actions of others. The Christian, the foundationalist, the Archimedean point seeker, places something or someone outside of the event. Against any sort of metaphysical urge, or desire to stand outside and above in order to judge, an existentialist, being unable and perhaps unconcerned with condemning the views and actions of others, does not necessarily imply apathy or relativism, rather it might imply equality. A metaphysical standpoint is harder to make consistent with equality. After all, how can people believe in equality if they also believe they stand outside and above other rational humans, or that a super-creature lives above us, or that there is a supernatural being you are privy to and others are not? Remember, the Christian attack is not an attack on those who have disregarded their humanity; rather it is an attack on those others who don't accept the Christian doctrine. The others could be virtuous in every other way, yet Christians feel justified, in their unwarranted arrogance, to see themselves as outside and above. The fact that one does not take seriously the virgin birth, the resurrection, the second coming etc. is not seen as a sign of rationality, rather it is interpreted as a sign of inferiority. Sartre points out that existentialism gets mistaken for naturalism simply for arguing that people are naturally free, passionate, rational, and responsible. Sartre's naturalism is a good, optimistic type of naturalism. He points out that traditional naturalists, such as Zola, who believe that man is but an animal, and a base animal at that, cause much less of a fuss to the Christian consciousness than his philosophy does. And it's largely his atheism that scares them. So, again, this is a metaphysical disagreement. Unlike Christians, who thinks humans are broken, are products of original sin, and unlike Hobbesian naturalists who think we are nothing but violent mammals, Existentialism puts free will, reason, passion, and responsibility at the center and sees them as talents. As talents they are things humans have within themselves and things they can develop further over time. Freedom is a talent. Sartre's Existentialism is the highest articulation of atheism and as such is closest to transcending the God/atheism binary.

The Christian critique is really a misunderstanding. Existentialism is not naturalism; it is humanism. It does not view us as mere animals that are wretched and can never change. Why the confusion? What really seems to be going on is that these critiques seem to be annoyed that existentialism is not afraid to struggle against power, to resist authority, to challenge past experience, and to do so without any care for a foundation. Christians and Communists held serious institutional and psychological power in Sartre's day; he challenged their privilege, and they resented him. They resented that Sartre was not content to just say "it's only human!" when someone did something repugnant. Where the Christian blames original sin and the Communist looks to the Party, Sartre had a more nuanced critique. What really scares the anti-existentialist is that existentialism "leaves to man a possibility of choice." The anti-existentialist is the anti-humanist. The anti-existentialist wants the individual to trust God or the Church or the Party or the State or the Dogma. Go into a typical church in America and you will hear church goers belting out — "trust and obey, for there's no other way to be happy in Jesus, but to trust and obey." These types of flights from freedom and responsibility, these aestheticized mantras, show how sinister this power is.

7

Both the Communist and the Christian critiques of Sartre's existentialism miss the mark because Sartre's existentialism is against atheism and against theism; it is against any conceptual foundation or mere idea. It is for choice and action. Both the abstract and concrete dualisms — God/atheism and Christian/Communist — rely on the idea that essence precedes existence, they rely on an idea or theory. They are mere beliefs, but do not see themselves as beliefs, so those who identify with them suffer from reification. Against any essentialist starting point, existentialism begins with the idea that existence precedes essence, but it is not so straightforward as to what this means, especially since Sartre does invoke the Cartesian cogito.

Existentialism has a quasi-Cartesian starting point including: the "je pense, donc je suis"; the centrality of consciousness; and the recognition of our isolation. Descartes takes the "I am, I exist" as the primary state of being human, but the problem here, as Husserl showed, is that this "I am, I exist" is a secondary, reflective state that is only possible at a certain level of development. It is not a foundation, not epistemologically, temporally, or conceptually. It relies on hidden assumptions, is the result of a dialectical process, and is not a stagnant given. Self-consciousness is not consciousness. One must reach a certain level of awareness, and knowledge, before one can reflectively and consciously objectify oneself. Existentialism realizes that pre-reflective consciousness is primary. Actually unconsciousness is primary. We begin as babies with no notion of who or what we are. We, over time, develop more and more awareness and consciousness. But we don't will thoughts, actions, and desires during these early stages of awareness. Rather thoughts, actions, and desires seem to happen to us, arise in us, and seem to have a life of their own. As Lacan showed, most of what is pumping through us, driven linguistically, are the desires, wishes, dreams, and needs of our parents, culture, and society. Becoming a self is not to start with a blank slate. As Sartre often put it, people must learn to "think against themselves" to become themselves. There are many hurdles here. There are the linguistic, cultural, and social aspects of oneself that one must first recognize and then either accept or reject.

Throughout most of our lives our primary way of being-in-the-world is pre-reflective. Philosophical dualisms, especially subject/object and theory/practice dualisms, are not primary categories when we are acting in the world. The big upshot of all this is that there is no primordial self and no soul lurking behind our thoughts, actions, and desires. There are just thoughts, actions, and desires which, with practice, if we are fortunate, we can control from time to time. In any case, as these thoughts, actions, and desires become habit and regular we can experience and see a human self emerging, and we can begin to understand what we care about and why we care about it and then, perhaps, freely choose or un-choose certain actions. Existence precedes essence.

8

Still existentialism is subject to the critique that human solidarity gets lost in the mix. From the communist side one could develop the argument that existentialism misses Hegel's point about the individual only being an individual because of others and misses the ways we are subject to the confines of history. And from the religious side, one could argue that a Cartesian starting point, the cogito as starting point, unjustly decenters God and others. Both the communist and Christian could argue that existentialism decenters human solidarity in favor of varying degrees of solipsism. A cogito based philosophy then must be careful to not naively assert "cogito ergo sum" as something immediate. Even the "I think, therefore I am" is mediated through history and dialectics. It must be understood dialectically and historical and not treated as an ahistorical truth. When it is taken as a foundational belief both the communist and religious critiques have some merit. To think of Descartes's cogito as the first brick of knowledge is naïve. It's problematic to think it unproblematic. To avoid the problems we need to introduce the idea of mediation. Consciousness is always already the result of a dialectical moment, a contrast of foreground and background; it is not simply the defining attributes of a concept. "I think, therefore I am" is only self-evident, if it is self-evident to you, because you are a self that has achieved a level of education, experience, and socialization so that the statement makes sense to you and you agree with it. Yet it still might not be true, and if it is true it is not foundational, or in-itself; rather its truth depends on relations between a subject, a world, others, and language. To take the Cartesian phrase as a starting point is fine so long as we recognize and acknowledge we are ignoring certain preconditions and making various assumptions. Start there if you wish but know it's not the starting line. The starting line has been wiped away so that it takes a leap of faith to believe that to doubt one's existence proves ones existence. The leap of faith may take the form of: there is a thinker required for there to be thought or it might be the assumption that language and logic can be trusted although they sometimes deceive us or it could be the assumption that you are actually thinking. To say that one knows one exists because one is thinking or is thinking because one exists, is something one could doubt. One can even doubt being merely "one." In any case, the point is that the cogito is not an Archimedean point; it is the result of a dialectical process; it is as much creation as discovery. As an invention or creation then, when we each articulate "je pense, donc je suis," we do become something we were not before that moment. In this way the foundation is interactive, as the idea that one exists is predicated on knowledge of existence outside the self and prior to reflective consciousness.

9

Just as the self before recognition is different than the self after recognition, the concept and object, the material self and idea, exist in dialectical tension. In this way each of these dualisms has meaning and existence only as they connect to each other. When Descartes discovers himself as a thinking thing he also discovers himself as a material thing. He is a thinking *thing*. We are part of nature and nature is material. Thoughts require language, language requires intersubjectivity, and intersubjectivity requires materiality. Put differently, thought requires language, language requires subjectivity, subjectivity requires intersubjectivity, and all of this requires a world for it to grow in. Our bodies, our brains, and perhaps our eyes, mouths, ears, and hands, are the conditions for dialogue. Language and thought are things that can be measured, written, heard, spoken, and created through action. No one without a body ever had a thought. No body, no individual, no self, every existed outside a world. No one learned a language without others.

And we should add that no thinking existed outside of history. Consciousness is mediated by history, society, the individual's experience, and in a sense, God. Consciousness is always consciousness of something. Besides concrete material differentiation, people also create contrast through abstract concepts. The Big Other, God, the Universal, or whatever abstraction helps provide the contrast that makes human consciousness possible and makes historical continuity viable and intelligible. Descartes's philosophy, in existentialism's hands, becomes historical and bridges both subject/object dualism and theory/practice dualism, within the action of articulating "I think, therefore I am."

10

Sartre defines existentialism as "a doctrine which makes human life possible, and, in addition, declares that every truth and every action implies a human setting and a human subjectivity."[1] As Richard Rorty famously put it, "You cannot crawl out of your own skin." But today we are getting to the point where perhaps you can. At the computer screen, on Skype, with your avatar or through robotics, we are seeing the first big push of transcending the body. But notice we are not transcending a human setting or human subjectivity. All roads lead back to us. We need to unpack the depth, because it is complicated by the fact that there are two kinds of existentialists: Christian and atheist. To get to the truth of existentialism we will have to transcend its meaning in both the Christian and atheist garb. The dialectic then proceeds from the idea that "existence precedes essence" or "subjectivity must be the starting point." We must not forget though that the starting point is not the beginning.

The idea of existence preceding essence offers a powerful interpretation when dialectically played against essence preceding existence. Sartre offers the idea of a paper-cutter as something in which the essence precedes the existence. With a paper-cutter someone first conceives of an object that will cut paper. The paper-cutter originates as an idea, and often the idea arises because there is a problem, or puzzle, or something lacking in the world from the standpoint of the person conceiving of the idea. Someone conceives of something he or she lacks or finds lacking in the world. As such, this person experiences the nothingness of existence and tries to fill that nothingness. That person creates a paper-cutter. When the person creates the paper-cutter, it is created with the intention for it to work a certain way and for it to be used in a certain way. The value and meaning of the paper-cutter stems from the idea the creator had, and the object is judged valuable or meaningful to the extent that it corresponds to the idea. If the paper-cutter cuts the paper as successfully as one wants it to, then the paper-cutter is valuable and meaningful. As Sartre puts it, the essence is "the ensemble of both the production routines and the properties which enable it to be produced and defined," and these precede the paper-cutter's existence.

11

Let's take another example. Some people prefer cats and others dogs. When people have a pregnant cat, they know before the mother gives birth that she will have kittens. The kittens will chase mice and birds, scratch,

---

1 All of my quotations in this section from Sartre are from *Existentialism and Human Emotions*, pp. 10–13.

hiss, meow, and only really listen and come to the owner when the cat food box is shaken. A pregnant dog, though, will give birth to something very different. Puppies will chew on things, bark, need to be taken on walks, and the so-called owners will have to scoop up their poop. In any case, cats and dogs have natures that we can anticipate before they are born and that we either like or don't like. We think their nature will sustain throughout the animals' lifetime. If a cat chases a mouse, no one is surprised and no one thinks the cat consciously decided to chase the mouse. It is just what cats do; it is in the cat's nature to chase the mouse. Existentialism, as typically articulated, concedes that artifacts and animals have essences that precede their existence. But existentialists claim humans are unique. On the one hand, similar to cats and dogs, we can describe what will appear after a woman gives birth. Babes in general do certain baby things. But on the other hand, there comes the moment when humans can be more unpredictable than other creatures. First, we change radically throughout history, both individually and socially. Second, we do judge human actions in ways we don't judge other animals. We don't just say "that's what people do" when someone kills an innocent person. To continue with the analogy, we can say that the traditional story is that God first had an idea, God wanted to create intelligent creatures but keep them away from the tree of knowledge, keep them in the dark, hide, and judge them. The point is that if God created humans, then we can be judged by how well we correspond to God's idea of us. We are good, or we have valuable and meaningful lives, to the extent that our lives correspond to the idea God had of us and the plan God had for us. In this way our essence precedes our existence. As Sartre puts it: "The concept of man in the mind of God is comparable to the concept of paper-cutter in the mind of the manufacturer...God produces man, just as the artisan, following a definition and a technique, makes a paper-cutter. Thus, the individual man is the realization of a certain concept in the divine intelligence."[1]

But then Nietzsche had to come along and spoil everything. Nietzsche said "God is dead." Without God, without someone or something to conceive of us beforehand, we have nothing we are supposed to correspond to. We are just born, we exist, and whatever we make of our lives will solidify, so to speak, and create our essence. Our essence comes after our existence. Our existence will create someone, over time, with regular and predictable behavior, and eventually it will solidify into an essence. It's complicated since freedom allows for choice, for irregular and unpredictable behavior, for complete reinvention, and even self-annihilation. I suspect a lot more people consciously kill themselves every year than dogs do. And, of course, cats think they are too cool to commit suicide.

---

1 Ibid., p. 14.

12

Nietzsche said "God is dead," not "God does not exist." The existential point is that when people believe in God, they very well might have a duty to ask what God wants from them. If God exists, we should find out what God wants. If God doesn't exist, then perhaps we need to ask if someone or something else had already conceptualized or conceived of us. Did nature, genetics, aliens, the universe, a mad scientist, our parents, or anything else conceive of us before we were born, and if so, do we have a duty to try to live our lives corresponding to the predetermined essence? The God/atheist dialectic often gets stuck on this question. But with "God is dead" Nietzsche is trying to signal that we should transcend this dualism. Nietzsche makes it clear that the death of God is more than the death of God. It is a metaphor for the death of any essence, including an "atheist" essence. When we transcend the dualism by rejecting the search for our essence, we do not fall into relativism; rather we have the opportunity, the duty perhaps, to create ourselves from within our moment of history. According to Nietzsche, then, the so-called "true world—we have abolished. What world has remained? The apparent one, perhaps? But no! With the true world we have also abolished the apparent one."[1] To push this even farther we can say that Nietzsche wanted to deconstruct, not just the idea of humans having essences, but also dogs, cats, and artifacts. Objects don't exist in some independent realm outside us. We are part of nature. As part of nature we are connected to the world and always already interpreting, coming from a perspective, and connected relationally; we are not independent or anterior or isolated atoms. Objects, both natural and social, don't have existence in themselves, they don't have some independent space outside of the world, and they don't have one true essence about them, while everything else about them is false. The conceptualization of dogs, cats, and artifacts was dialectical, which is partly to say creative, from the start, and Sartre's existentialism needs to address this. We will have to go beyond Sartre's articulation to get to the truth of this.

13

The understanding of atheism that is most attached to theism comes out of 18th-century philosophy. That version of atheism discarded the notion of God but not so much the notion of essence preceding existence. Diderot, Voltaire, and Kant and other 18th-century philosophers all conceived of a human nature, a nature found in everyone. Individuals are all a particular example of a universal concept, *man* (as they liked to put it). Even in Kant the

---

1 Nietzsche, *Twilight of the Idols*, p. 51.

essence of human beings precedes our existence. Today's popular atheists, from Dawkins through Harris, follow the 18th-century definition of atheism and with it the idea of an essence.

Contrast this with the view of Sartre. As Sartre sees it, if God does not exist, or better yet, if God is dead, "there is at least one being in whom existence precedes essence, a being who exists before he can be defined by any concept, and that this being is man."[1] In other words, according to Sartre, first we just turn up, we appear on the scene, and only afterwards do we define ourselves. At first we are nothing; we become something, and we ourselves make what we will be. There is no human nature and no God to conceive us. "Not only is man what he conceives himself to be, but he is also only what he wills himself to be after this thrust toward existence."

If existence precedes essence, then Sartre can claim that "Man is nothing else but what he makes of himself." He calls this the first principle of existentialism since it is an articulation of existence preceding essence. He also calls it subjectivity. Unlike a stone or a table, we hurl ourselves toward a future and are conscious of imagining ourselves in this future. "Man is at the start a plan which is aware of itself...man will be what he will have planned to be. Not what he will want to be." If this is the case, we are responsible for what we become and, according to Sartre, we are responsible for everyone since there is no one else and nothing else to pass the buck to. Once we are conscious of our responsibility, then we can only deny it at our own peril. To forget our freedom and responsibility is to be immature, it is to live in "bad faith."

14

When Sartre talks about subjectivism, he is talking about more than just the ability of a subject to make choices and create itself. Self-creation is important, but beyond that one of the distinguishing features of existentialism is the idea that there is an asymmetrical relationship between subject and object. Adorno would claim that the priority goes to the object. Objects are primary, since objects seemingly can exist without subjects, while every subject is also an object. Sartre's philosophy challenges this. It seems like common sense to say objects exist without subjects, but actually any object we cite by definition is not independent of subjectivity, for we are citing it. As citing it, we are putting something of ourselves in it. We are active by virtue of being alive and so we contribute to any object we touch, see, or think. Any object we are aware of is either physically experienced or

1 All of my quotations in this section from Sartre are from *Existentialism and Human Emotions*, pp. 15–16.

thought of through the mind. In this way no object exists without a subject. In this way priority goes to the subject.

To say objects exist without subjects to experience them or think them is to fall into Kant's trap: insisting there are noumena, things-in-themselves, and then claiming we cannot know them. By talking about them at all, Kant is implicitly claiming to know something about them (that they cannot be known). To borrow a phrase from Habermas, this is a performative contradiction. In the act of "performing" the claim that there are noumena, one says something about noumena. Sartre is aware of the issue here, so he simply labels the world prior to consciousness, or outside consciousness, "being-in-itself," but leaves it at that.

Existentialism doesn't deny that there is a world beyond what humans have experienced. The world is larger and older than us. But they deny that there is a world that is in principle unknowable to us. And they deny that anything can exist "in itself." Nothing is in principle unknowable because we come to know the world through our actions, and we can "act" on anything. And there is nothing completely separate and independent, because everything in the world exists in relation to other things, as relations to other things; everything is in the world with everything else. There are not objects in the world that interact with nothing but themselves; there is just a world, and everything in it is always already interacting. In this sense then there are no "natural" objects, there are simply multifarious possible relations. The world is dialectical.

In fact we can say there are really no objects in themselves because the things interacting are not things. What is meant by this is that they are not simply one thing. There are many ways to divide up the world; there is not just one way to divide up the world. In this way there are no essential objects. The smallest unit of reality then is a relation, not a thing. As human subjects we construct relations that matter. Our relations matter because consciousness allows us to freely choose relations we want. In other words, from a variety of choices we can act as we wish; we are not programmed. Sartre insists we always have a choice, even in seemingly unfree situations. We can hold our breath, fight, run, blink, etc. Our relations also matter because we can also interpret in creative ways. We are condemned to choose and interpret. When we accept this, we are being authentic and taking responsibility for ourselves and our world. When we do this, we begin to create knowledge and to have knowledge.

We are pushing into dangerous ground here, and we need to be wary of falling into idealism or naïve humanism. But Sartre's philosophy stresses materialism. The relations we create stem from material actions. It is materialist because to observe, interpret, and differentiate is a material action. It is the action of a human being, and human beings are physical beings. Thoughts too have a materiality about them. The mediation between subjects and the world always occurs through a physical being interacting with a material world. The claim here is not that we take in the whole world all at once, nor is it that things don't happen outside of us, but rather it is that there is no one "true" world independent of us and unaffected, in principle by us. There is nothing standing above us. It is not our duty to try to carve up the world in the way it wants to be carved up. It is only we who bring values and interests to the world. Perhaps, then, objects only exist as relational entities, and subjects are needed to form the relations or make the differentiations. Still we can say objects are outside us, in that there are parts of the world we have not interacted with, but they are not outside us in any metaphysical sense. We are part of the world, and it is part of us. There is no metaphysical dualism, no difference in kind. There is only one kind, there is only one world.

15

We see then that when Sartre talks about subjectivism, he is making a rather radical claim. There is no transcending human subjectivity, and this is the "essential meaning of existentialism."[1] If there is nothing outside us defining us, then we are responsible for ourselves, for others, and for the world. But this responsibility is not an idea or a thought; rather it is an action. As active subjects we are creating all three through our actions and we are always acting. To be or not to be is still the existential question. Still, we might reframe it as "to breathe or not to breathe." We can look at this from two aspects. To take in breath or to hold one's breath is not the question, for both are actions. In both cases one is still being, existing, and hence interacting in the world. But to breathe or end breathing through death triggers the existential condition. Only in this latter case will a subject's action cease. To hold your breath or not hold your breath is still to act. But when you cease to *be*, when your breathing permanently ceases, your action also ceases. But so long as one is being, we are condemned to interact, interpret, and create, even if that only means to breathe or hold one's breath.

In articulating this Hegelian interpretation we need to keep two things separate. First there is the typical Hegelian move that asserts contrast. The famous example we saw in Chapter 2 is that when we posit being, it quickly gives rise to nothing. Each term generates a negation of itself, which it is internally dependent on, and, if we are lucky, it generates a positive move in the dialectic. This is why it seems ingenuous when some, like Terry

---

1 Ibid., p. 17.

Eagleton,[1] who are trained in Hegelian–Marxism, claim that their belief in God is not instrumentally driven but is driven by an intrinsic need to answer metaphysical questions such as "Why is there something rather than nothing?" The obvious Hegelian answer is there is nothing. Also there is something. It could not be otherwise. There couldn't be nothing unless there was also something; there is something and that is why there is nothing. We are something and that is why we can be nothing. And as we saw in Chapter 1, being nothing doesn't and can't mean simply nothing. Nothing contains being and being contains nothing. Asking "Why is there something rather than nothing?" is as interesting as asking "How many angels can dance on the head of a pin?" These are questions only someone with a bad metaphysics could waste time with. The conclusion Eagleton should have drawn, rather than jumping to God, is to make nonsensical metaphysical questions nothing. Or since Eagleton is witty and good, he just could say "my bad."

16

In the case at hand, being and nothing generate becoming. *Being and Nothingness* is the title of Sartre's master work so we should take this as a hint as to the importance of dialectics for existentialism. But there is another, more fundamental, aspect of dialectics that I am arguing is internal to Sartre's existential philosophy, whether he is explicit about it or not. This other aspect is closer to Adorno's sometimes use of dialectics. It's not similar to his later negative dialectics but it is similar to his earlier use of determinate negation in *The Dialectic of Enlightenment* (with Horkheimer) and his *Minima Moralia*. In *Dialectic of Enlightenment* Horkheimer and Adorno give the example of a tree. Again, we can link this with Sartre's phenomenology of a tree in *Nausea*. In *Dialectic of Enlightenment* the point is that a tree, named as an individual object, is just tautological. One name, one thing. Dialectically it's also not tautological. It's an object and a word. To steal from Magritte and Foucault, *Ceci n'est pas une pipe*. The word tree is not a tree (even if it names just one thing). When we give a conceptual definition of a tree, we think of it as really listing the attributes which make a tree a tree. Whether or not these attributes are the "natural" or "essential" ones, if we all agree on the definition we have a concept "tree" and can apply it to different individual trees. But the point Horkheimer and Adorno make is that any particular conceptualization is not necessary. Some definitions are better for some situations and others are better for other situations. There is not one conceptual definition that transcends us. Conceptualization doesn't capture some higher, or essential, truth. Conceptual definitions are one way of interpreting the world. They are not necessary, higher, or automatically

1 See Eagleton, *Reason and Revolution.*

more true than other ways. And they are not outside history. Yet, dialectically, the concept tree comes into being as the individual object; the specific tree becomes what it is not. Both the object tree and the concept tree are only what they are as they are becoming what they are not. The concept is an idea, and perhaps a theory. The object is a thing, it is material. But in both cases it is a practical act, an active subject that is creating the differentiation. The naming and differentiation of the object and the theoretical linking of the object to other objects, real and imagined, is a practical act, a choice. In this way the most fundamental insight of dialectics is to point out a double asymmetry. First, we have the subject/object dualism where the object only becomes that object because of a subject differentiating it in a creative action. By becoming, though, I don't mean we are responsible for actually creating it (although we often are; we create lots of stuff), but we partly determine how the world is sliced up. But it's always mediated by history and the world's materiality. Subject/object dualism gives way to active subjectivity. Second, we have the theory/practice dualism which subsumes the subject/object one, since the object has already been subsumed into subjectivity without becoming mere subjectivity. We recognize the second asymmetry when we see that the theory is, theory exists only because of an active, material subject conceptualizing it as such, and then proves the theory in action. In other words, theory is dependent on human practice. Theory is a practice of a creating subject. In this way practice proves or validates theory. Theory/ practice dualism gives way to reflective practice. This dialectical double-truth, the solving of subject/object dualism and theory/practice dualism, is the radical, hidden truth within existentialism.

17

Taking this back into the concepts that directly drive existentialism then, we can say that existentialist dialectics, as the practice of determinate negation, can posit an origin such as the cogito, knowing that it means not merely a thinking thing, and not simply a theory, and not unsophisticatedly solipsistic. The idea of a thinking thing tries to purge itself of being an entity, but it is only intelligible as an entity — it's a thinking *thing*. As such it holds objectivity since there is always an object or materiality being mediated. At the same time it refutes or negates subject/object dualism by always already staying attached to material subjectivity. Next it negates theory/practice dualism since the theory is only actualized, is only true, when actively pronounced. "I think, therefore I am" is an action necessitated theory. As a practice of an isolated individual, each alone must pronounce, and prove to oneself, "I am, I exist." Further, this solitary act tries to negate the notion of intersubjectivity; it claims solipsism, and yet it is a theory for any and all conscious and dialogic beings. All of us can perform this so-called solitary act; a solitary act that one probably learned from another. The action of stating "I am, I exist" is a theory for all conscious beings to know themselves and the theory only works if one articulates it; it only works as an action. One might think that it is proved true, is validated, when practiced, when articulated in isolation. Yet, this is not enough. Even Descartes recognizes that he could be crazy, he could be a madman. He wonders if he is like those insane people "whose brains are impaired by such an unrelenting vapor of black bile that they steadfastly insist that they are kings when they are utter paupers."[1] So he writes books, he engages others in dialogue, for that is the only way to test truth claims. We can only validate our existence, and validate any truth claim (or to use metaphysical language—ground existence and truth) in and against others in dialogue.

To bring this directly back to what interests Sartre, he would say that when I choose myself I do so materially and actively as a subject, and choosing it as a subject is to understand that everyone else also does so as material and active subjects. The image of the human comes only from "the humans" (as Trump might say) so that when anyone chooses him or herself he or she is creating an image of what it means to be human, and there is no other image of the human except ones that come from us. Neither God nor nature-in-itself offers us a vision of the human. Neither nature nor God speaks. Only people speak, engage in dialogue; only humans articulate statements with truth value. Only between each other do we discuss, argue, and come to consensus; we carry normativity into the world through our language. We are the creators of normativity and in this sense we are affirming the value of whatever we choose. It is in this sense that Plato was correct in stating that we always choose the good. We speak the good, we choose the good, and "nothing can be good for us without being good for all."[2] What Sartre clearly means here is not that everyone should literally choose what we choose, but that what we choose is a legitimate option for others — for others are also active, free subjects. And if others disagree, we can talk about it, discuss it. This component makes existentialism a humanistic philosophy. Dialogue becomes central because, since we are always putting ourselves into the world, we need to discuss with others so we don't colonize the other, or falsely project. Through dialogue we can hold each other accountable, test

---

1 Descartes *Meditations on First Philosophy*, p. 14.
2 All of my quotations in this section from Sartre are from *Existentialism and Human Emotions*, pp. 17–18.

our truth claims, and have a better sense of what's inner and what's outer. Dialogue, then, is an essential art of being human.

The image we create and fashion "is valid for everybody and for our whole age." For what we choose affects others and sets the conditions for where others will have to live their lives. If I choose to marry and have children, it involves all humanity since I am creating the idea and reality of humans who marry and have children. Our choices become patterns and get solidified and institutionalized as more and more people choose the same. As Sartre puts it: "In choosing myself, I choose man." We can try to flee from this, as when Charles Barkley famously declared, "I'm not a role model." Barkley can state that, and it might be his belief. But in reality it is false. Barkley was a role model. Other humans, and especially young athletes, mimicked him. Truth is not an idea or opinion or theory; it is concrete reality, it is an action. Sartre is closer to the eastern philosophy of Confucianism that emphasizes responsibility than he is to Charles Barkley. And Charles Barkley should read Bishop Berkeley. To be is to be perceived, and when perceived, one becomes a model. It's not under the control of the perceived, rather it's the perceivers who decide whom they see as role models. If you don't want to be a role model, hide.

18

Sartre famously declared that "man is anguish."[1] Anguish is the feeling we experience when we recognize our radical freedom and the burden of choice that comes with it. As we have seen, it is a feeling of total responsibility. We are responsible for ourselves, others, and the world. No wonder we would want to flee it at times. After the death of God, you see people dreaming of aliens, and UFOs, and artificial intelligence to ease our anxiety. If creatures from another planet show up, or AI develops in such a way that we have someone or something greater than us, bigger, faster, stronger, smarter than us, we can be relieved of anguish and anxiety. God is not dead. God is death. Any post-God god is just another urge for, and fear of, death. It is an attempt to avoid anguish. But for the existentialist, anguish can be useful for getting us to recognize the truth of the human condition. Emotions are contradictory. On the one hand we feel bad for someone who is suffering anguish. On the other hand, if you are suffering anguish it could be a good thing. It might be the condition of possibility for you to seize your humanity. In this way emotions are beyond good and evil. Emotions too are caught in the dialectic. It sounds innocuous when someone says you should get in touch with your feelings. It's supposed to be a positive thing. Yet as an existential act, getting

---

1 Ibid., p. 18.

in touch with your feelings might result in anguish, fear, trembling, shame, and forlornness. It could be a prescription for years of therapy. The dialectic then would move from stoicism to deep feeling (or vice versa) and then into actions that control the emotions. The first two steps in the dialectic reify emotions or lack of them, while the third step of choosing your emotions demystifies them until you see them not as controlling you, but recognizing you are controlling them.

19

If our actions create legitimacy, create our world, and even create our emotions, then we have entered a Kantian paradox. It is a paradox because the Kantian construction exists but without the Kantian grounding. Existentialists still ask what would happen if everyone acted as one is acting — not because one has a fundamental duty to reason but because in acting, each is intrinsically legitimating the action, as the action legitimates each of us. Existentialists don't turn to a duty outside the self or to formal reason; rather they acknowledge a creative urge within the self. Reflective consciousness is the condition for our creative urge, an aesthetic impulse that values action because it is action conscious of itself. The action itself proves the value of the action. It's a closed circle only containing human choice. For example the act of lying "implies that a universal value is conferred upon the lie."[1] According to the existentialist there is nothing more to universalism. It might seem like a version of the "is implies ought fallacy," except it might not be a fallacy if there is no independent or anterior ought, outside the action itself. If ought just is another word for is, then it's not fallacious, it's tautological. If truth is an action, and the action exists, then the proof is in the pudding, so to speak.

To put this another way, when we ask ourselves if we have the right to act in such a way that humanity might guide itself by each of our actions the meaning of anguish starts to come into focus. Leaders feel this anguish, especially in military situations, but it doesn't lead to quietism; rather "it is the very condition of their action. It implies that they envisage a number of possibilities, and when they choose one, they realize that it has value only because it is chosen." If you claim it has value but don't choose it, then you really didn't value it. By the same logic, if you didn't do something you claim to value out of fear, then you didn't value that something as much as you valued fear. This is a tough statement but you can see why, in this sense, anguish too is part of the action itself and is partly explained by the responsibility we feel toward others. We feel responsible because we are

---

1 All of my quotations in this section from Sartre are from *Existentialism and Human Emotions*, pp. 19–21.

responsible, and we are responsible because we feel it. There is no grounding, but there is interplay between the particular choice and the universal. The universal exists because people existed before us and they gave the world value. We are born into their world and we interact with it. It is in us before we are conscious of it. As we interact we make it ours. We choose to continue valuing what they value, or we choose something else, we begin to create a new "universal."

20

What Heidegger called abandonment, Sartre called the forlorn. By forlornness "we mean only that God does not exist and that we have to face all the consequences of this."[1] Existentialism is not a secular ethics that tries to get rid of God without pain. Saying "God is dead" is not to celebrate the death of God. Without God, Sartre argues that there are no *a priori* values. A traditional secular ethics thinks that with the death of God nothing needs to change. We still can have our traditional values such as don't lie, don't kill, don't steal, etc. Against secular ethics and moral principles Sartre suggests that we must be consistent and abandon moral principles. What we have left are aesthetic values. Still, when understood correctly, these are appropriate for guiding our lives. The lesson to be drawn, for the existentialist, is that if God does not exist it is a big problem for morality, and for the notion of principles, because the "possibility of finding values in a heaven of ideas disappears along with Him." In other words, there are no Platonic forms because "there is no infinite and perfect consciousness to think it." Dostoyevsky's "If God didn't exist, everything would be possible" is another way of articulating the starting point of existentialism. This is just another way of saying existence precedes essence. Everything is permitted and so we are forlorn; we experience dread because nothing inside the self and nothing outside the self exists to adhere or conform to. In this way, Sartre says we have no excuses. Actually we never really did; everything has always been permitted. Now we are just being honest about it.

The upshot, as we have been saying, is that existentialism rejects determinism, even as we are not completely free. We did not freely choose our existence and our choices are not unlimited. Still we are "condemned to be free." Sartre makes this clear in his brilliant, and true, example of a student who came to him for advice. This poor student was torn between joining and fighting with the Free French Forces against the Nazis or escaping France with his mother. It was complicated by the fact that his brother had been killed by the Nazis and he wanted to avenge his brother's death. Also, his

---

1 All of my quotations in this section from Sartre are from *Existentialism and Human Emotions*, pp. 21–23.

father had become a collaborator, so he felt obliged to take care of his mother. What was the right thing to do? And is there any moral principle that could tell him? Sartre says no. He must simply choose, and choose knowing that he cannot control his ultimate fate. If he joins the resistance, he might fight extraordinarily and be the reason they defeat the Germans. Or he might die in training camp before he even sees action. On the other hand, leaving France with his mother may be the only thing that keeps her alive, or they might both die even so, or she might come to hate him and think him a coward. The point, though, is that theories such as Christianity, Kantianism, and Utilitarianism can't really help. Still, it's not completely correct to say that Sartre rejects moral principles. Principles can help guide us, but they should serve life; they are not determinate. They are guides that can help us navigate concrete situations.

Another excellent Sartreian example is the hypothetical case of a Jewish person fleeing the Nazis. This innocent person runs to your house, asking to come in since the Nazis are chasing her. "Of course," you say. Then the Nazis come to your door and ask where the woman is. You lie and tell them that she ran the other way and hid in the cemetery. You go inside and you tell your husband that the woman can come out now, and he tells you that the woman had doubts about the house being safe, so she ran away to hide in the cemetery. Unwittingly you have just told the Nazis where the woman is. The point is that life is richer than any theory or principle can capture. We must all make choices knowing that the consequences of our choices will transcend our motives and desires. The answer to this is reflection and more action, rather than flight from responsibility. Sartre valued truth telling, but did not turn it into a fetish. He also valued the usefulness of using probability reasoning, but he did not expect it to be a panacea.

21

What do we do? One might conclude that: "If values are vague, and if they are always too broad for the concrete and specific case that we are considering, the only thing left for us is to trust our instincts."[1] "But how is the value of a feeling determined?" What gives a feeling value is if it provokes action. If one feels something but doesn't act on it then the feeling loses something of its value. The only way to determine the value is to perform an act which confirms and defines it. The truth of the belief, the truth of what one values is proved in the action, in reality. In this way we know ourselves through our actions. And yet it's more complicated. It's hard to tell the difference between a true feeling and a pretend feeling. Putting on

---

1 All of my quotations in this section from Sartre are from *Existentialism and Human Emotions*, pp. 26–28.

an act is almost the same, for feelings are formed by the acts one performs. I cannot refer to it in order to act on it. "I can neither seek within myself the true condition which will impel me to act, nor apply to a system of ethics for concepts which will permit me to act." There is a continuum between faking and not faking, between bad faith and being authentic. In other words, even the dualism between bad faith and authenticity is problematic. At the level of belief or idea, we cannot be sure as to whether we really know ourselves. But through the action, and in the action, truth and self-knowledge emerge. It's not completely problematic. As one action becomes a pattern, becomes "natural" so to speak, authenticity grows. Authenticity involves knowing who we were, choosing what we want to be, and not claiming to have discovered a true self. And as we recognize that we are choosing, and admit we are inventing, we move deeper into authenticity. We start to know ourselves as our actions reflect it all.

And yet there is no way to ever know for sure. Because existence precedes essence, there is no object outside us, no self within us, which will absolutely validate or refute our choices. We can never completely know who we are because we are constantly in the state of becoming, and we are extremely complicated, and driven and pulled by a number of incalculable factors, desires, impulses, drives, and pressures. We play roles, sometimes we internalize them, and the world labels us and we often internalize these too. In this way the inner life is a product of the outer and an invention from the outside. This is why the existentialist journey is a long one. It requires bravely going forward, honestly looking back, and all the while acting with reflection.

Getting back to the student who asked Sartre for advice as to whether he should join the resistance or flee with his mother, what can Sartre, being Sartre, tell him? Sartre knows that asking a teacher or a priest or anyone you trust still doesn't absolve you of the responsibility. First, you don't have to ask anyone. And when you do ask someone, you are choosing whom to ask and choosing whether to accept the advice. Often you know how the person will advise you anyway, and so at some level you already know, more or less, what you are going to hear. It is you making the choice; you have decided what kind of advice you will get. Sartre told the kid, "you're free; choose, that is, invent." This is tough, but people seek out the advice they want to hear. Conservatives watch Fox News, liberals go on the Huffington Post, Catholics ask their priest, and college students ask existentialist philosophers.

22

A central issue related to choice is interpretation. Sartre articulates the complexity of interpretation by writing about a Jesuit he met when he was a prisoner.[1] As a child, this man's father died and left him in poverty He was made fun of in school, he failed in school, and at 18 he failed in a love affair. And if that wasn't bad enough, at 22 he joined the military and failed there, too! He interpreted all this into a story to make sense of his life. He took it as a sign to avoid secular success and to look to religion; he saw God in it all and entered the order. Notice how his life was not a story; he did not experience it as a story but only afterwards did he create a story to deal with his disappointing life. The idea of life as a story is popular today, but this example should serve as a warning against the idea that "life is a story." Life is not a story and, most likely, if you see your life as a story you are probably creating a fiction for yourself. Your story is bad faith. In the case of the Jesuit prisoner, those of us looking in from the outside see that he chose this interpretation to save himself; it was simply a coping mechanism. As Sartre says, he could have chosen to be a carpenter or revolutionist. If you have watched the television show "The Walking Dead," think about how the governor reinvented himself. People do it every day. Some know they are inventing, and others cannot face truth and so project a necessity or bigger agent behind the choice. Yet, as moderns, we all know God is not speaking to any of us; we alone are choosing. In this way "Forlornness and anguish go together."[2] We are thrown into this world, free to do practically anything, and condemned to determine what it means. People desire to make their lives into a story and they desire the feeling of being the author of themselves. But often the forming of a story is a fiction. It's a series of contingent choices and interpretations. In telling a story, one is not changing the actions but rather one is reinterpreting the actions to fit the narrative. This is dangerous because actions, the substantial materiality of our existence, go deeper into us than our beliefs. This becomes clear when we consider a simple example: what you actually eat, what you put in your mouth, affects your health more than what you believe about your health and more than the story you tell yourself concerning food.

The desire to make one's life a story is driven by the same desire to be part of a bigger story, part of God's story. Existentialism rejects these interpretations as metaphysical urges. These interpretations are inferior because they don't see that they are interpretations, inventions. Any story once told is necessary not contingent. When you pick up a book or watch a film, the story unfolds out of necessity because it has already been written or created. What the characters or actors do is already written in stone. If God exists, our essence precedes our existence, and our lives are written in stone. When we recognize that God does not exist, we lose the structure

---

1 See Ibid., pp. 28–29.
2 Ibid., p. 29.

of necessity and the contingency of our life appears. But even without God many still yearn for necessity. This can take the form of developing a materialist metaphysics in order not to experience despair. A science-based metaphysics that explains the universe may provide comfort if it is pitched as a story uniting the individual with the wide world. A science-based metaphysics is a religious metaphysics because it, like religion, posits truth and reality outside us. This is why one can be a scientist and also believe in God. A scientific-based metaphysics doesn't invoke the despair of an existential metaphysics. An existential metaphysics rejects God and Truth. Despair captures this. Existentialists let go of metaphysics since they realize metaphysical systems are untrue. If creation is central to epistemology and ontology, then one cannot discover metaphysical truth. Rather one must create knowledge and the world; projecting outside us is epic fear.

23

Sartre captures this attitude, saying: "We shall confine ourselves to reckoning only with what depends upon our will, or on the ensemble of probabilities which make our action possible."[1] He sees talk of faith, eternity, and metaphysics as avoidance behavior. Sartre defines concrete life as life connected to one's lifeworld. He gives the example of waiting for your friend to arrive by train. One must deal with probabilities that the train will run on time and so on. He suggests you disengage yourself when the probabilities go beyond your action: "The possibilities are to be reckoned with only to the point where my action comports with the ensemble of these possibilities." Because some things go beyond our will and control, Sartre finds Descartes's maxim "Conquer yourself rather than the world" motivating. This does not mean that people need to isolate themselves. Rather to "conquer yourself" is to control what you can control, and to work with and trust those who matter. As Sartre puts it, he relies on those "in which I can more or less make my weight felt." In other words, he counts on those he has influence with and those who care about him. This extends to the world we are part of. Similar to relying on the train to be on time, it's rational to rely on those you work with but nothing further. One cannot abstractly rely on the "goodness of man" or those on the other side of the planet, or future generations, and so on. Limit yourself to what you see. Use probability concretely because people can change, and you are less likely to notice if you are not engaged with them. It's an aesthetic skill; an art for knowing what to do, when to do it, whom to trust, and how to combine it all into a human life.

---

1 All of my quotations in this section from Sartre are from *Existentialism and Human Emotions*, pp. 29–30.

In this spirit the scientist need not give up on science. Science is the scientist's world, it is a scientific lifeworld. Scientists are part of the history and are creating and perpetuating it. The suggestion is not to give up science, in the same way one should give up God, but to acknowledge that science is a human creation. This does not diminish it, rather it makes it creative even as scientists attempt to discover the way the world is. They read the journals, talk to other scientists, work in the lab and this is how scientists can discover the way the world is. At the same time they can acknowledge that they are contributing to the way the science world is as they discover it. Science and scientists are not outside the process of knowledge, or the world they are "discovering."

24

Unlike the "the returned" from the French television show *Les Revenants*, Sartreian others are only hell while alive. Dead people do not speak. And we can add that speaking, or language in general, following Chomsky, is aimed first and foremost at understanding, aiding thinking and creating, not simply pragmatic communication. In this way existentialism agrees with Chomsky by starting with "I think, therefore I am." This is consciousness being aware of itself; this is language creating a human self. Without language an existentialist individual or even a Cartesian person doesn't come into existence. And ironically, because of language, we also doubt our existence, and make up supernatural beings, as well as pretending there is an essential self hiding behind the doing self, and so on. In this way the dialectics of language often outwits us and make us lose ourselves even as it is the condition for us to be selves at all.

Existentialism then puts human dignity, the notion of a robust organic self, and interacting with others, at the forefront. While traditional materialism treats us as any other object in nature, existentialism's use of subjectivity, finds others in the cogito. We cannot escape others. We reach the "I think" in the presence of others and others are just as real to us as our own self. Others are the condition for our own human existence and the condition for us to recognize this human existence. To get to a truth about oneself, one must have contact with another person. The "gaze" can aid one in seeing the truth. Seeing how our actions affect others, and how they react, can help us understand the truth of a situation. On the other hand, if the gaze of the Other is too strong, too dominant, it can provoke neurosis, fear, and an unhealthy attempt to mimic or please. As such one can lose the self, miss truth, and feel less than human. The gaze is a trap as well as a condition for emancipation. It exposes the truth of a continuum between a self and others, rather than a dualism, and yet this continuum can feel more dualistic than the deepest dualism. In the same way that we can only feel terribly distant from someone we are close to, we can only truly feel ourselves as individuals because of the gaze of the Other. The most famous conceptual example to clarify the relationship between an individual and others that Sartre gives is that of shame. The fact that we feel shame proves that others exist. To sense one's human self is, at the same time, to sense other selves. Growing up alone on a desert island, one would not experience oneself as a human self, let alone articulate "I think, therefore I am." We don't need language to communicate to others, but we need others to communicate to ourselves. Because of others, we develop language that allows us to go deeper into ourselves.

It's like a game of basketball, where someone must inbound the ball so another can dribble it up court, but this other doesn't dribble the ball up court. The other's presence and actions allow one to get the ball and move, and the other's presence allows one to get language to think and to recognize a self. In this way when one discovers the other, one discovers one's self, and when this discovery happens it dialectically reflects and "proves" the other as well. Intersubjectivity is necessary for subjectivity. We don't have to take this as far as Habermas (but we could) and claim that argumentation aimed at understanding is more fundamental than argumentation aimed strategically. In any case, it does agree with Habermas's insistence on giving priority to subject/subject relations over subject/object ones. Without intersubjectivity we could not manipulate objects in a human sort of way. Our human selves only develop through a material thinking self. The social and the biological organically come into existence together, and evolve together. They are not atomistic; they are intersubjective. And it is through our intersubjectivity that we create ourselves and our world, including the creation of a thinking self and an active creator.

25

If subject–subject relations are a condition for subjectivity, then we can say that there is a human condition even if there is no human nature. Our human condition is the scope and the limit of our biological and historical selves. In this way our condition is both subjective and objective. It is objective because intersubjectivity is found within all subjects, and it is subjective as all subjects live out their particular lives. This should give us hope for solidarity because other human lives will never be completely strange to us, as the human past is never completely strange to us. We always have a point of mutual reference. Still, our universality, the ability to understand others is not given but is "perpetually being made."[1] The cogito ties it all together.

The way the existentialist sees it, there is and there is not progress. There is progress in the sense that we live in the world as we made it. We might make the world better or we might make the world worse, but in either case the world is what we make it. If we make gay marriage legal, it will stay legal unless homophobic others change the law. There potentially is progress in the sense that history unfolds because of what we do. But in another sense there is no progress. There is no teleology that everyone is aiming for, nor is there teleology in the world, nor is there an eschatology that everything is moving toward. Further, there is no progress because every individual must create an individual life. Even if there is advanced knowledge in science and math available at one's time in history, the individual must still learn the science and math for herself. One must create oneself, for one is born pretty empty; one starts life as a baby and must go through stages of development. The path of growing up will be an individual path but it will also be on the larger path forged by those who came before and driven by the given point in history. This is what Sartre means by existentialists don't believe in progress: progress is betterment, but man is always the same, only the situation confronting him varies; choice always remains a choice in a situation.[2]

In one sense there will be no progress in the God/atheist choice because everyone must decide for themselves, but there will be change, and one can hope there will be progress. It depends on how history plays out. If you are born into a world where no one believes in God, that's where you start from. Where you will go with it is not written in stone. Since today most people are born into families and communities that tell them that God exists, it takes effort to overcome the falseness of it. Telling children that God exists puts them at a disadvantage when it comes to truth. They start their life with a handicap, a fiction that they will have to work out of if they want freedom.

But since there are no facts that can end speculative debates once and for all, the situation is more complicated than it may first seem. Our relation to the world is one of interpretation. We do not interact with the world from a position of absolute truth or even from an objective or factual position. We are always situated in the world and we always come to the world from a specific perspective. One might think this is a disadvantage but it is actually an advantage, it's the condition for truth. If we were robots or AI, then interpretation would be a disadvantage, but since we create truth through our actions, interpretation and choice is what gives us freedom. If we could not interpret and choose, we could not create; rather we would just

---

1 Ibid., p. 39.
2 Ibid., see p. 44.

follow our programming. We would not have knowledge, we would have no human subjectivity.

26

But to say we must interpret, for we are more than programs, is to say also that we can fall off track in a way a program cannot. We can forget we are interpreting and we can mystify and reify ourselves and the world. According to Sartre's philosophy, when we mystify and reify we are interpreting faultily. We are lying to ourselves and are committing bad faith. Some interpretations are better than others. Those in which we recognize ourselves as interpreting are better than those that mystify and reify reality. Still, in another sense it doesn't matter. Everything is arbitrary, everything is equal. Whether we reify or not, we are still the actors; and since there are no pre-established values floating around in the world, then moral choice and any choice is more akin to an aesthetic decision than anything else. When one creates a work of art, there are no *a priori* values one must follow; but after one makes the art work, then it can be judged. In this sense it is initially arbitrary; there was no necessity to what you created, yet this does not make the completed artwork arbitrary, as it was created with your intention. As an individual creation, it carries your style. Style only exists though individuals, yet it transcends them. Art and morality have creation and invention to them. When a student makes a choice, it is not insignificant for "in choosing his ethics, he makes himself."[1] It would only be irreducibly arbitrary if there were one correct answer that exists before the decision is made. But without God, we have to invent values. Our actions always already create value, often unwittingly. Life has no meaning *a priori*.

We can see the two senses then when we look at how Humanism itself breaks into two meanings. The first meaning claims that humans are higher in an abstract sense. Just by virtue of being human we might think we are higher or greater than the rest of nature. Religion teaches this. Existentialism does not accept this because it would imply a value to all individuals, either because value was bequeathed by God, or because of the prior deeds of certain people. Sartre warns us that the notion of "Mankind" is a dangerous abstraction. In other words, it is dangerous to think that just because humanity has created so much that an individual gets to take credit for it by virtue of being human, or just because of having been born. That would be like children expecting respect and credit because of what their mother and father accomplished. This is a confusion of self and others. But the second meaning of humanism is different. The second meaning is that one partly is outside the self, always projecting beyond, and pursuing

1 Ibid., p. 43.

transcendent goals, and because of this one is able to exist in a human sense. Transcendence is a constituent element of being human, not in the sense that God is transcendent but in the sense of passing beyond one's given subjectivity. This meaning of humanity stresses constant action, interaction, and emerging possibilities to create with will and consciousness.

27

Sartre is an atheist but he makes it clear that although existentialism is atheistic, it "isn't so atheistic that it wears itself out showing that God doesn't exist."[1] Even if God existed, that would change nothing. Again we have to look at this in two senses. In one sense, of course it would change things. If God existed we would have to calculate that into our lives. But in a deeper sense it would not matter. If God gave us free will, if God could give us free will, we would still be forced to choose and to interpret. There would still be contingency and freedom. Here, finally, we see Sartre getting beyond religion and atheism. It's tricky though because he needs to keep the language of theism and atheism in order to be intelligible to his audience. And yet, to move beyond God and atheism will require the action of discarding that language. This is not easy, it is not individually accomplished.

God is the emptiest of all concepts and yet humans have endowed it with the highest meaning. "Man is the being whose project is to be God."[2] In the end then, in the big picture perhaps, God is a metaphor for the metaphysical urge, for the urge to be free and yet have things happen by necessity. God is our contradiction as we are a contradiction. The desire to be God is a desire to reach beyond our finite, contingent, and limited selves to something necessary. At the same time, God is a desire for prefect freedom. In this way, God is a diversion, but a dangerous one since God doesn't exist. But also that is why we can move beyond God.

Some people, rather than going to church, play golf for diversion. Pascal said we all have the desire to be diverted. Pascal is surely correct because if the desire for diversion was not in us, golf would not exist, because golf is patently absurd. Pay lots of money to hit a ball, get frustrated, hit the ball five more times, and then tap it into a hole. Waste oceans of water keeping the fairways green, and waste a lifetime waiting behind a tee and walking or driving a silly little cart for eighteen holes. In itself, golf is stupid. But anyone who plays seriously and enjoys golf sees more in the sport. Golf forces one to focus; it helps one set concrete goals; it provides distraction and stress relief; it can help build human relationships; it's a puzzle that cannot be perfected. It is a diversion and it is more than a diversion. It can be transcendent. Golf

1 Ibid., p. 51.
2 Ibid., p. 63.

is a concrete activity that reaches beyond itself. You have a better chance of getting hit by a golf ball than being struck by God. Fore!

28

Finally, Sartre emphasizes that existentialism rejects the "spirit of seriousness."[1] This spirit has two characteristics. One is that it considers values as transcendent, it sees them as outside subjectivity; and second it takes desire, which is an ontological category stemming from our freedom, and makes it a simple material constitution. For example, it says we desire bread because it is necessary to live and bread is nourishing. But this is bad faith, an attempt to flee anguish. And Sartre couldn't be more right. In the United States, to desire bread is to experience anguish. But not for existential reasons: it's not because we wish to deny our freedom. It is much simpler than that. Bread in the States is lousy! It is either clay-like so-called Wonder Bread, or heavy wheat bread, or hard as rock pseudo-baguette. Trying to get decent bread here will give one the experience of anguish.

Beyond this, Sartre's point is important. When we think that values are somehow outside us we are giving priority to ideas. We try to get our beliefs to correspond to some perfect or objective idea outside us; we deny our freedom. The perfect is the enemy of the good. We see students judged by adults, telling them they must be perfect, must get a 4.0, and must have perfect attendance, and so on. We should strive for excellence, not perfection. The urge for perfection is the urge for a dangerous metaphysics. Perfection is a stagnant concept. It's an impossibility for a rich, contingent, contradictory being. This is why language is important. Words such as "perfection" sound great in theory but are often misguided. They also hide menacing desires in aesthetic garb. The desire for perfection is sinister and a distraction in a quest to make oneself and those who matter proud. It's an immature desire designed to sidestep the human condition.

Desires get invented like everything else. When we think our desires are a simple consequence of the world we deny our freedom. When we think we desire bread because it nourishes us, we are canceling out the moment of freedom. Against these flights, Sartre's point is that when we experience anguish it means we are beginning to recognize that we must invent values, choose to live or not, choose to be nourished or not, and we must decide what we will eat to nourish us, or even decide if it's worth it to eat at all. This anguish, when we face it honesty, prompts us to see that we must be serious and not serious. When we take ourselves too seriously, we are acting as if things are necessary, and we are forgetting that ultimately nothing matters. At one level it doesn't matter what we do. One day we are going to die and

---

1 Ibid., p. 92.

lose everything. This is why Sartre can say that getting drunk alone or leading a nation amounts to the same thing.[1] On the other hand, if we are not somewhat serious, we will waste the time we do have. We will never have our moment. We will have squandered our life if we do nothing just because we resent not getting everything. Today we are not dead, so our choices do matter. Despite the impossibility of living a perfect life, Sartre lived his life to the fullest; he lived an excellent life. We can say without contradiction, then, that his life was more meaningful and not more meaningful than the guy down in Venice Beach with the cardboard sign that says "world's greatest drunk."

---

1 See Sartre, *Existentialism and Human Emotions*, p. 94.

CONCLUSION

1

One could imagine (especially if Mormon) Jesus growing up around Venice Beach and going back to his ten-year class reunion. Everyone is asking each other what they have been doing with their lives. Some have gotten married, some have children, many have started new jobs or earned higher degrees; some have moved out of the area and others, unfortunately, have died. But what about Jesus? When asked, Jesus says, "I found out I'm the son of God and so I started a Jewish cult." Of course, he would be the laughing stock of the reunion.

The Bible never mentions Jesus's adolescent years, so you know he was troubled and an underachiever. We all know that one guy who was the most annoying in high school, and he comes back for the ten-year reunion full of stories and really trying to convince everyone that he is somebody. They should make a Jesus movie, staring the sometimes anti-Semite Mel Gibson, in the spirit of *Romy and Michelle's High School Reunion*. Which is the bigger fib? Claiming to invent Post-It or claiming to be the inventor of everything posted? Of course the larger Jewish community knew Jesus since he was a snotty-nosed little brat with long hair, so they are not surprised at his tale; they are simply amused. Still, some don't even remember him at all. But even the annoying, story-telling kid can get a dozen other slackers to follow him. While Jesus couldn't sell his claim of being God to his people or his community, good old Paul was able to pawn it off on some non-Jewish suckers, and the rest is history.

Seeing a Christian weep over the thought of Jesus is just strange. Clearly this was just a guy who hadn't found himself yet. He was hanging out with harlots, perhaps going to strip clubs, and he knew he wasn't going to have anything to show for the fifteen-year reunion, so he had to stage something. Nothing like staging a resurrection to get people to notice you; and saying, like Schwarzenegger in *Terminator*, "I'll be back" adds a pretty cool aesthetic flair to it. If only the class officers in his school had the sense to skip the fifteen-year and just plan for the twentieth, Jesus might have had time to become somebody. Nietzsche is probably right in saying that if Jesus had lived another decade, he would have given up the whole supernatural thing. He did have quite a few cool ideas, mainly socialist ones, and he seems like a guy one would want to eat fish with. But the way his life (and non-return) actually played out makes it hard not to be amused when I see my fellow Californians driving SUVs with "Jesus Freak" or "Not of this World" plastered on the back window. Now, that's chutzpah! It gives me the same chuckle as when I'm in San Francisco and I see a white guy who grew up in Orange County sitting in the park talking about Buddhism and meditating. Namaste.

2

As it becomes less and less plausible to accept a supernatural metaphysics, religious arguments have taken on a different form. Since the metaphysical arguments and empirical evidence are nonexistent for God, Jesus as son of God, and every other prophet or supernatural event, a lot of religious people and some sappy philosophical and religious scholars talk about "the religious experience." They do this because they have lost the war when it comes to the metaphysical and epistemological issues. Suddenly they say evidence and logic are not important, and whether or not one can prove God exists is beside the point. What matters, we are told, is the religious experience itself, and the effect and meaningfulness it fosters in the believers. Of course this is a perfect example of bad faith. The scholars make a fuss using silly words such as "awe," when they should really be at the doctor saying "aaahhh" so they can become well. We know what drives the charlatans publishing and preaching to the masses.

Beyond that, we know that what drives supernatural beliefs and so-called religious experiences are basically three things. First, religion stems from the cry of terror in the face of the unknown. Terror prompts the mind to misinterpret nature as something supernatural. When the preponderance of nature is too complicated to assimilate into one's understanding, the primitive or frightened human mind misunderstands it as coming from the outside, coming from something beyond the nature they are accustomed to. New perceptions can cause misinterpretations especially when fear is involved. If one interprets what they see as under the hand of a supernatural agent one can hope to survive in the face of the overwhelming. Perhaps the supernatural being, unlike brute nature, will spare you. Horkheimer and Adorno convincingly argue for this in *Dialectic of Enlightenment*. Coping with the fear of death is a simpler way to explain it. Second, religion is a way to feel special. It's a narcissistic and immature mode of being that hides its truth in "the religious experience." As Horkheimer stresses in *Eclipse of Reason*, this becomes obvious with the dominance of Christianity. One might think the Christian individual is small and helpless, since the price of salvation is self-renunciation.[1] Yet individuality is bolstered by the belief that earthly life is just a fleeting moment in the story of the eternal soul. The individual is strengthened by the notion of having an individual soul and the possibility of living for eternity. A sense of equality with God develops because God created man (and woman, to a lesser extent) in his own image, and Christ's atonement for our sins provides a substantial link. Christianity emphasizes the idea of the soul as an inner light, a place of God. In this way it gives individuals a sense of greater worth and individuation. There is incentive to interpret keystone experiences in one's life as "religious experiences." The language of the pious help create the religious experiences. The favored phrases here are — I'm trying to get closer to God — oh, what a creator! — it only matters what God thinks of me — such is the power of God! — I've got to thank the Big Guy for that. The awe-inspired language of religion constructs a mind that, often without realizing it, is selfish and juvenile while feigning superiority, depth, and ethical interest. It relieves many people of the existential weight of existence and adulthood. Third, as Feuerbach showed, religion is ideological. It is a belief that rationalizes, distorts, and reflects the greater economic reality. It is used by the ruling classes to exploit and control the masses. At the same time, though, it holds up higher values and virtues. Ultimately, it distorts love, human potential, human solidarity, human creation, and human labor. In turn individuals become distorted but don't see or feel it, since their group suffers the same disease. Racists don't feel like racists around other racists. The point is that the ingenuousness or neurosis within the believer, when wedded to social norms, makes the ideology stick. As a group delusion, it gains the semblance of normalcy and legitimacy. All three reasons are dialectically intertwined and believers (as well as non-believers) have some of all three within them, as they are all embedded into our world today.

As the advocates of religion have moved from metaphysical arguments to a subject's experience the ability to challenge these irrationalities becomes more difficult. The notion of shared experiences and consensus gives way to subjective feelings and "my truth." This fragmented, individualistic language,

1 See Horkheimer, *Eclipse of Reason*, p. 92.

religious experience language, is a product of our stage of capitalism. It's a stage of fragmented people under the spell of a globalism they cannot grasp. Everyone senses the totality but mislabels it as metaphysical when it is simply the modern world we created. The irony is that now more than ever is the time to talk about totality and yet religious experience language is by definition personal and atomistic. As isolated, subjective reason is an unwitting tool to support irrationality. When religion claimed to be grounded in metaphysical argument, it appealed to a shared reason, intersubjective, and communicative. It appealed to a reason that any thinking person could contemplate. With the emphasis now on religious experience, though, the idea of God is now attached directly to faith and atomistic subjectivity. This frees believers from the need to validate their so-called religious experience with knowledge and gives license to sidestep communicative discourse. As such it becomes shamelessly instrumental, anti-knowledge, and pro-faith. It becomes dangerous and immature. It simply provides the means to believe what one wants to believe, regardless of truth, history, or consequence. It gives free rein to incoherent interpretations and so is perfect ideology for our incoherent age of global capitalism that wants to be obeyed but not seen. Stripped from any need for justification or consensus, it exemplifies irrationality and injustice. It mirrors the given world. Religion has come full circle. Blinded by a world beyond comprehension we invented religion, blinded by incomprehensible religion we cannot see ourselves, we cannot capture the totality.

3

We can see the difficulty in capturing the totality by looking at the difference between being able to describe an event and actually understanding the event. We can watch a basketball game and describe what statistically happens on the court. We can record the shots, assists, turnovers, rebounds, and fouls. When we become familiar enough with the team, we may even begin to predict what will unfold, what plays will be run and who will win the game. We could also program an AI to record and catalogue all this. But it is something entirely different to watch a game with understanding, to know the game and to understand how the game operates within our society. To watch a game, as game, within the totality, is radically different from watching through the lens of mere statistical analysis, or for betting, or for fantasy league, or for show, or to be seen. Only the former captures what it means to feel, experience, and be the game. And only the former has the potential to, at the same time, understand the regressive and progressive aspects that the game reflects concerning American society. A true fan, a person who understands the game of basketball, has a very different experience and understanding than those who are at the game simply because they want to be entertained or because they have deep pockets. A true fan understands the game and what it means. Further, to understand the value of basketball in our society is another thing altogether. To capture the meaning of the game of basketball and to develop a theory that produces understanding of the game, ourselves, and our society that controls the game, is an action that transcends what one learns from sitting in the bleachers collecting stats or selfies. We could throw an AI into the bleachers, have it record the game and such, but it cannot think and figure out what it means. And it cannot think, reflect, choose, or act.

Theists and atheists are comparable to those non-fans, those privileged or deluded people (or AI) sitting in the bleachers watching, recording, a game. They can describe their beliefs and record the game of religion, the game of God. Their ideology gives them tools to predict and control aspects of the world. Yet they lack understanding because understanding is a different sort of activity; it's an activity that situates ideology within the mode of production. Understanding requires recognizing the subject's construction of the game and the fact that the game only exists because people have made it up and given it power. Outside of us religion doesn't exist; God doesn't exist. Yet religious people cannot see this because they believe in an objective supernatural world outside and above our human one. Atheists are stuck reacting to an imaginary game. Atheists argue over who actually is winning and what the true stats are. Atheists need to reject the game. Just because one has a ticket to a game doesn't mean it's worth going to the game. But habits are hard to break and giving up power is not easy. Saying "I'm a Christian" or "I'm an atheist" is an angle granting power and privilege in today's world. These identities colonize our society, and yet these labels are no more meaningful than people saying they are Raiders fans or Star Wars fans. Actually Raider fan or Star Wars fans have the advantage of following something culturally modern, and the disadvantage of following a mere commodity. In any case, in the game of God, there is a hero and a villain for both theists and atheists. Still, the fight for the individual's soul within this game results, no matter which side wins, in commodified and reactionary identities that cannot offer authentic meaning or value. The irony, though, is that since these ideologies are so embedded in our world, they make one better equipped for success. In wrong society the people who truly understand the meaning of the game of God are at a disadvantage. Those with the advantage should not be proud. In wrong society, wrong people thrive. The Spotlight is rarely on them. Those playing for or against God thrive in our society. These ideologies provide clarity to those who cling to them.

4

Today it can be confusing to think beyond God and atheism. This mental confusion might be the sign that the falseness of both is coming to light. In the preface to the new edition to *History and Class Consciousness* Lukács says, "Mental confusion is not always chaos. It may strengthen the internal contradictions for the time being but in the long run it will lead to their resolution."[1] Following Lukács, we have seen that a dialectical approach doesn't just discard false concepts, such as God and atheism, rather: "Concepts which are false in their abstract one-sidedness are later transcended [zur Aufhebung gelangen]. The process of transcendence makes it inevitable that we should operate with these one-sided, abstract and false concepts. These concepts acquire their true meaning less by definition than by their function as aspects that are then transcended in the totality." In this way one can say "in so far as the 'false' is an aspect of the 'true' it is both 'false' and 'non-false'."[2] Socrates, Descartes, Marx, and Sartre offered clues to the transcendence of both God and atheism, and they did so to the extent that they rejected metaphysics for dialectics.

Lukács says a dialectical analysis differs from a metaphysical one in that with dialectics "the definite contours of concepts (and the objects they represent) are dissolved."[3] Unlike the "one-sided and rigid causality" of metaphysics, dialectics emphasizes interaction and specifically interaction between subject and object. And we should add theory and practice. With metaphysics "the object remains untouched and unaltered so that thought remains contemplative and fails to become practical; while for the dialectical method the central problem is *to change reality*."[4] Without dialectical insight conceptual analysis becomes subject to the reified terms of society. The result is a one-sided interpretation. As we have seen, in the dialectic between God and atheism, one side of the misinterpretation is fatalistic. God, as omnipotent, omniscient, and omnibenevolent must have a plan and nothing and no one can alter it. It's God's world and we are just living in it. The other side of the misinterpretation can be seen in what Lukács calls "voluntarism."[5] Voluntarism is a naïve understanding of free will. It thinks that thoughts alone have power. It thinks rejecting something false equates with truth.

Atheists think their rejection of God eliminates God and provides them with a course for living in the world. The world stripped of God will open the door to truth. Individuals who buy into voluntarism think they just can do

---

1 Lukács, *History and Class Consciousness*, p. xi.
2 Ibid., pp. xlvi–xlvii.
3 Ibid., p. 3.
4 Ibid., p. 3.
5 See Lukács, *History and Class Consciousness*, p. 4.

what they want if they stick to what can be seen. Yet, it's more complicated than this. Truth is not achieved through correspondence, and atheism is just a negative concept, and, as such, can be filled with anything and longs to be filled with something. This makes atheists susceptible to the contemporary ideology. Today religious people and atheist folk are trapped in the dialectic between fatalism and voluntarism and are "necessarily complementary opposites, intellectual reflexes clearly expressing the antagonism of capitalist society and the intractability of its problems when conceived in its own terms."[1]

5

Philosophy is against religion and against atheism as it rejects mere ideas, false notions of identity, and epistemological and metaphysical claims that posit knowledge as passive, and a world ontologically outside us. Still, one does not simply discard beliefs that have such social and historical power. As social and historical powers they contain parts of our better selves hidden within the mystified ideas and reified reality. Philosophy becomes more than negation, more than critique when it acknowledges itself as an action and engages power. As a reflective action it fights against power and ideology and pushes back against actual existing reality, even as it cannot see the future clearly. This should not scare us, though, for lack of clarity can be a good sign. One need not rush toward clarity, as clarity can be a way to hide lack of understanding.

Transcending God and atheism is not a panacea. It will not guarantee us a true or good world. Still, rejecting the false dialectic will help us recognize that the world is our construction and our responsibility so long as we are here. We will never experience a world outside our created world. Would there be a world if we were not around to act on it, to think it, and to experience it? Perhaps. But we are here and so ontologically part of the world. Can we exist without the world? Can the world exist without us? Can a text exist if you take out a central character? In one sense no, because then it would be a different text. Can the world exist without us? Not this world. It would be a different world. Nothing exists but this world, our world.

Nothing is beyond God and atheism. Why not become nothing? Make yourself and those who matter proud.

---

1 Ibid., p. 4.

BIBLIOGRAPHY

Adorno, Theodor. *Aesthetic Theory*. Robert Hullot-Kentor, trans. Minneapolis. Minnesota Press. 1997.

———. *Minima Moralia*. E. F. N. Jephcott, trans. London. Verso. 1994.

———. *Negative Dialectics*. E. B. Ashton, trans. New York. Continumm. 1992.

Allen, Woody. *Irrational Man*. Sony. 2016. DVD.

Arato, Andrew. "Lukács's Theory of Reification." *Telos* 11. Spring 1972.

Arato, Andrew and Paul Breines. *The Young Lukács and the Origins of Western Marxism*. New York. Seabury Press. 1979.

Aristotle. *The Basic Works of Aristotle*. New York. Random House. 1941.

Badiou, Alain. *Theory of the Subject*, Bruno Bostells, trans. London. Continuum. 2009.

Baudelaire, Charles. *Flowers of Evil*. New York. Dover. 1992.

Berliner, Alain. *Ma Vie En Rose*. Sony. 1997. DVD.

Berman, Marshall. *Adventures in Marxism*. London. Verso. 1999.

Bernstein, J. M. "Lukács Wake: Praxis, Presence, and Metaphysics." *Lukács Today*. Rockmore. 1988.

———. *The Philosophy of the Novel*. Minneapolis. University of Minnesota Press. 1984.

Browning, Christopher. *Ordinary Men*. New York. Harper. 1998.

Brudney, Daniel. *Marx's Attempt to Leave Philosophy*. Cambridge. Harvard University Press. 1998.

Callinicos, Alex. *Against Postmodernism*. New York. Saint Martin's Press. 1989.

———. *Social Theory*. New York. New York University Press. 1999.

Cohen, Jean, L. and Andrew Arato. *Civil Society and Political Theory*. Cambridge. The MIT Press. 1992.

Davis, Walter. *Death's Dream Kingdom*. London. Pluto Press. 2006.

Descartes, *Meditations on First Philosophy*. Donald A. Cress, trans. Indianapolis. Hackett Publishing.1993.

Donovan, Thomas. *Dialectic of Enlightenment as Sport*. New York. Algora. 2015.

Eagleton, Terry. *Culture and the Death of God*. New Haven. Yale University Press. 2014.

———. *Ideology*. New York. Verso. 1991.

———. *On Evil*. New Haven. Yale University Press. 2010.

———. *Reason, Faith, and Revolution*. New Haven. Yale University Press. 2009.

Feenberg. Andrew. *Lukács, Marx and the Sources of Critical Theory*. Oxford. Martin Robertson. 1981.

Feuerbach, Ludwig. *The Essence of Christianity*. George Eliot, trans. New York. Prometheus Books. 1989.

Freud, Sigmund. *Civilization and Its Discontents*. New York. W. W. Norton. 1989.

———. *The Future of an Illusion*. New York. W. W. Norton. 1989.

Foucault, Michel. *Discipline and Punish*. Alan Sheridan, trans. New York. Vintage Books. 1977.

Fukuyama, Francis. *America at the Crossroads*. New Haven. Yale University Press. 2006.

———. *The End of History and the Last Man*. New York. Free Press. 2006.

Gershoff and Grogan-Kaylor, "Spanking and Child Outcomes: Old Controversies and New Meta-Analyses," Journal of Family Psychology, April 7, 2016.

Gogol, Nikolai, *Dead Souls*. New York. Vintage. 1997.

Habermas, Jürgen. *Between Facts and Norms*. William Rehg, trans. Cambridge. MIT Press. 1996.

———. *Between Naturalism and Religion*. Cambridge. Polity Press. 2008.

———Habermas and Joseph Ratzinger. *The Dialectics of Secularization*. San Francisco. Ignatius Press. 2005.

Hall, Stuart. *Modernity*. Cambridge. Blackwell. 1996.

Harvey, David. *The Condition of Postmodernity*. Cambridge. Blackwell Press. 1990.

———. *The Limits To Capital*. New York. Verso. 1999.

Hawking, Stephen. *The Grand Design*. New York. Bantam Books. 2010.

Hegel, G. W. F., *Elements of the Philosophy of Right*. H. B. Nisbet, trans. Cambridge. Cambridge University Press. 1991.

———. *The Encyclopaedia Logic*. Indianapolis. Hacket Publishing. 1991.

———. *Phenomenology of Spirit*. A. V. Miller, trans. Oxford. Oxford University Press. 1977.

Heidegger, Martin. *Being and Time*. San Francisco. HarperSan Francisco 1962.

Hollis, James. *Why Good People Do Bad Things*. New York. Avery. 2008.

Homer. *Iliad*. Stanley Lombardo, trans. Cambridge. Hacket Publishing. 1997.

———. *Odyssey*. Stanley Lombardo, trans. Cambridge. Hacket Publishing. 2000.

Honneth, Axel. *Reification*. New York. Oxford. 2008.

Horkheimer, Max and Theodor W. Adorno. *Dialectic of Enlightenment*. Edmund Jephcott, trans. Stanford. Stanford University Press. 2002.

Horkheimer, Max. *Eclipse of Reason*. London. Continuum. 2004.

Jameson, Fredric. *Marxism and Form*. New Jersey. Princeton University Press. 1971.

———. *The Political Unconscious*. New York. Cornell University Press. 1981.

Jay, Martin. *Adorno*. Cambridge. Harvard University Press. 1984.

———. *The Dialectical Imagination*. Boston. Little, Brown and Company. 1973.

———. "Habermas and Modernism," in *Habermas and Modernity*, ed. Richard J. Bernstein. Cambridge. MIT Press. 1991.

———. *Marxism and Totality*. Berkeley. University of California Press. 1984.

Kant, Immanuel. *Critique of Pure Reason*. Norman Kemp Smith, trans. New York. St. Martin's Press. 1965.

Kellner, Douglas. *Critical Theory, Marxism and Modernity*. Baltimore. John Hopkins University Press. 1989.

Khatchadourian, Raffi "The Doomsday Invention." The New Yorker November 23, 2015.

Kierkegaard, Soren. *Fear and Trembling*. London. Oxford University Press. 1939.

Kundera, Molan. *The Art of the Novel*. Linda Asher, trans. New York. HarperCollins. 2000.

———. *The Curtain*. Linda Asher, trans. New York. Harper. 2006.

———. *The Festival of Insignificance*. Linda Asher, trans. New York. Harper. 2015.

———. *Ignorance*. Linda Asher, trans. New York. Perennial. 2002.

———. *Immortality*. Peter Kussi, trans. New York. HarperPerennial. 1991.

———. *Slowness*. Linda Asher, trans. New York. Harper. 1996.

———. *The Unbearable Lightness of Being*. Michael Henry Heim, trans. New York. Harper. 1984.

Lahiri, Jhumpa. *In Other Words*. Ann Goldstein, trans. New York. Knopf. 2016.

Lee, Bruce. *The Tao of Jeet Kune Do*. New York. Black Belt Communications. 2011.

Lefebvre, Henri. *Critique of Everyday Life*. John Moore, trans. New York. Verso. 1991.

Lukács, Georg. *A Defense of History and Class Consciousness*. Esther Leslie, trans. London. Verso. 2000.

———. *History and Class Consciousness*. Rodney Livingstone, trans. Cambridge. MIT Press. 1971.

———. *Marxism and Human Liberation*. New York. Dell Publishing, 1973.

———. *Soul and Form*. Anna Bostock, trans. Cambridge. The MIT Press. 1971.

———. *The Theory of the Novel*. Anna Bostock, trans. Cambridge. MIT Press. 1999.

Mandel, Ernest. *Late Capitalism*. Joris De Bres, trans. New York. Verso. 1972.

Marcuse, Herbert. *Eros and Civilization*. Boston. Beacon Press. 1966.

———. *One-Dimensional Man*. Boston. Beacon Press. 1964.

———. *Reason and Revolution: Hegel and the Rise of Social Theory*. Boston. 1960.

Marx, Karl. *Capital* vol. one. Ben Fowkes, trans. New York. Vintage Books. 1977.

Marx, Karl and Frederick Engels. *The Communist Manifesto*. Samuel Moore, trans. New York. Washington Square Press. 1964.

———. *Economic and Philosophic Manuscripts of 1844*. New York. Prometheus. 1988.

———. *The Marx-Engels Reader*. New York. W. W. Norton. 1978.

Nehamas, Alexander. Nietzsche: *Life as Literature*. Cambridge. Harvard University Press. 1985.

————. "Nietzsche, modernity, aestheticism." Bernd Magnus and Kathleen M. Higgins, *The Cambridge Companion to Nietzsche*. Cambridge. Cambridge University Press. 1996.

Nietzsche, Frederick. *The Portable Nietzsche*. Walter Kaufmann, trans. New York. Penguin Books. 1982.

————. *Twilight of the Idols and The Anti-Christ*. R. J. Hollingdale, trans. London. Penguin Publishing. 2003.

Nothomb, Amélie. *The Character of Rain* St. Martin's Griffin. 2003.

Offe, Claus. *Contradictions of the Welfare State*, ed. John Keane. Cambridge. The MIT Press. 1993.

Ollman, Bertell, *Alienation*. Cambridge. Cambridge University Press. 1976.

Onfray, Michel. *Atheist Manifesto*. Jeremy Leggatt, trans. New York. Arcade Publishing. 2007.

Plato. *The Trial and Death of Socrates*. Indianapolis. Hackett Publishing. 2000.

Rorty, Richard. *Contingency, Irony, and Solidarity*. Cambridge. Cambridge University Press. 1989.

————. *Take Care of Freedom and Truth Will Take Care of Itself*. Stanford. Stanford Press. 2005.

Roy, Olivier, *Holy Ignorance*. New York. Columbia University Press. 2010.

Samuell, Yann. *Love Me If You Dare*. Paramont. 2004. DVD.

Sartre, Jean-Paul. *Existentialism and Human Emotions*. New York. Citadel Press. 1985.

————. *Literature & Existentialism*. New York. Citadel. 1977.

Sciencemag.org September 11, 2014 and November 5, 2015.

Schopenhauer, Arthur. *The World as Will and Representation*. E. F. J. Payne, trans. New York. Dover Publications. 1969.

Shakespeare, William. *The Complete Works*. New York. The Viking Press. 1986.

Taylor, Charles, *Hegel*. Cambridge. Cambridge University Press. 1975.

Vogel, Steven. *Against Nature*. Albany. State University of New York Press. 1996.

————. "Marx and Alienation from Nature." *Social Theory and Practice*, Vol. 14, No. 3, Fall 1988.

————. *Thinking like a Mall*. Cambridge. The MIT Press. 2015.

Voltaire. *Candide*. London. Penguin. 1947.

Warnke, Georgia. *Gadamer*. Stanford. Stanford University Press. 1987.

———. *Legitimate Differences: Interpretation in the Abortion Controversy and Other Public Debates*. Berkeley. University of California Press. 1999.

Wiggershaus, Rolf. *The Frankfurt School*. Michael Robertson, trans. Cambridge. The MIT Press. 1994.

Žižek, Slavoj. *How to Read Lacan*. London. Granta Books. 2006.

———. *Less Than Nothing*. London. Verso. 2012.

———. *The Puppet and the Dwarf*. Cambridge. The MIT Press. 2003.

———. *The Sublime Object of Ideology*. London. Verso. 1999.

INDEX

Made in the USA
San Bernardino, CA
15 August 2016